Practical

Wicca

The Easy Way

Practical Wicca
The Easy Way

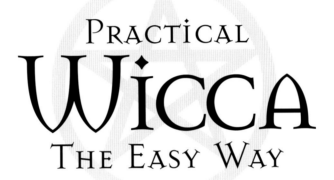

Christine Seville

Sterling Publishing Co., Inc
New York

Creative director: Sarah King
Editor: Clare Haworth-Maden
Project editor: Yvonne Worth
Designer: Axis Design Editions
Limited

Library of Congress Cataloging-in-
Publication Data Available

10   9   8   7   6   5   4   3   2   1

Published in 2003 by Sterling
Publishing Company, Inc.
387 Park Avenue South, New York,
N.Y. 10016

This book was designed and produced
by
D&S Books
Cottage Meadow, Bocombe, Parkham
Bideford, Devon, EX39 5PH

Distributed in Canada by Sterling
Publishing
C/o Canadian Manda Group,
One Atlantic Avenue, Suite 105
Toronto, Ontario, Canada M6K 3E7

Printed in Singapore

Sterling ISBN 1-4027-0587-5

CONTENTS

Introduction

Introduction

Most of us have grown up with an image in our minds of what a witch looks like, normally an ugly, wicked old crone, dressed in black robes and a pointed hat, armed with a book of evil spells and a broomstick, and always accompanied by her ever-faithful black cat.

This misconception was born out of the anti-witch propaganda of the Christian Church as it tried to suppress the practices and religions of the past. Even until relatively recently, witches were portrayed as evil villains in such movies and fairy stories as *The Wizard of Oz* and *Sleeping Beauty*.

Thankfully, the perceived role of the witch has now started to change from that of a villain to a wise and honorable hero or heroine, as seen in television series like *Sabrina, the Teenage Witch, Bewitched,* and *Buffy the Vampire Slayer,* and movies like *Harry Potter and the Sorcerer's Stone* and *The Fellowship of the Ring* (although these movies tend to focus on wizards rather than witches). As a result, people are now beginning to regard practitioners of magic as decent and wise, thereby helping to reverse centuries of persecution and distrust.

Despite this change in perception, however, most people still consider witches to be people who should be feared and loathed, overlooking the fact that most witches are very honorable people with high moral values that would put many modern-day religions to shame.

ABOVE *This typical image of a witch is one we learn at an early age.*

So who, or what, is a witch, and what does it mean to be a Wiccan?

The Wiccan faith can trace its practices back for many thousands of years, and most likely derives its early roots from the animal cults and shamanistic belief systems of Stone Age Europe. These animal cults formed the core of many of the faiths of early human society, and helped our ancestors to begin to understand the patterns of the natural world, leading them to a basic psychological understanding of themselves and the world in which they lived.

The tribal shaman would explain complex ideas and concepts through the symbolism of the natural world, including animals, seasons, changing weather patterns and stars. In time, these cults developed some very sophisticated beliefs about magic and religion, and although their names and interpretations varied throughout the world, the symbolic meanings behind them were virtually the same in every civilization and culture. This is one of the main reasons why the Wiccan faith has seen such a revival in the last century: its symbolic meanings are familiar and relatively easy for everyone to understand.

ABOVE *Our ancestors began to notice patterns, not just in the world around them, but in the stars in the night sky.*

ABOVE *The symbolism of the Wiccan faith is similar to that of other faiths and cultures throughout the world, the only possible exceptions are some eastern cultures that use 5 elements instead of 4.*

In times past, the old ways and beliefs were passed on through word of mouth because the people who were told them couldn't read or write. These legends, which were changed and adapted by many different cultures over time, were generally remembered through stories, songs, and nursery rhymes, and were rarely recorded, although some examples have been found in the form of runic or hieroglyphic symbols in tombs and temples. These examples are evidence of the first written language, but few people are able to understand or interpret them, even today.

ABOVE *The wisdom of many ancient religions survives in runic or hieroglyphic symbols. These cryptic images are examples of the first written languages.*

Wiccan deities

Although Wiccans worship and honor many deities, or lesser gods, and elemental lords, their focus of worship is on the "divine creative force" (resembling the "great spirit" in Native American tradition), which is subdivided into the male and female principles of the God and the Goddess (similar to the Chinese concept of yin and yang). As well as making up the divine creative force, these two opposing forces, or aspects of nature, can be subdivided into further deities, many of whom were proclaimed saints by the early Celtic Christian Church.

The God

The God is the masculine force, the master of life and death. In pagan belief, the image of the Horned God (or god of the hunt) is a very powerful symbol, which, despite having been used by the Christian Church to represent the devil, is, in fact, far from evil, representing, as it does, only the darker side of nature. Cave paintings dating back to about 30,000 B.C. have been found in France showing depictions of the Horned God.

ABOVE This powerful image of the Horned God has over the centuries been misused by the Christian faith to represent evil and to condemn the Wiccan faith.

LEFT The tradition of the bride dressing in white stems from the pagan Goddess worship and symbolizes the purity of the virgin bride.

In many pagan wedding ceremonies, the groom would wear antlers to represent the Horned God. Even Edward the Confessor, the famously pious king of England, is thought to have followed this pagan practise so that those of his subjects who still followed the old ways would acknowledge his wedding. The bride, on the other hand, would dress in white, sometimes also wearing either a semi-circular crown, symbolizing the new moon, or a crown of flowers, representing the Goddess. Even to this day women traditionally wear white dresses in which to get married.

The Goddess

The Goddess is the female, or light, side of nature, equivalent to the Native American Mother Earth, who represents the caring and nurturing aspects of life. As Mother Nature and the mother of all things, it is her power that controls the seasons and brings the rains that feed the earth. Indeed, Goddess-worship was once fundamental to the farming year because, while the God was directly equated with the power of the sun, the Goddess was identified with the more subtle force of the moon, a force that influences the seasonal weather changes that farmers count on for high crop yields. The moon, which often symbolizes the Goddess, is also the power that controls the tides and is known to affect the emotions of

ABOVE The Image of the Goddess can be linked to the cycles of the moon and the seasons of the year (see page 29).

many people (see page 29), and it is significant that emotions are generally associated with women rather than men.

The worship of the Goddess teaches us about the three phases of life—childhood, adulthood, and old age—through association with the three phases of the moon—new, full, and old. The phases of the moon are also linked with the three phases of womanhood, the new moon representing the virgin or maiden, the full moon symbolizing the mother, and the old moon signifying the old woman or crone.

BELOW LEFT The Goddess symbolizes the caring and loving qualities of mother nature.

The origins of Wicca

Although Wicca can trace its origins back to the belief systems of the Stone Age peoples of Europe, it is more than merely one faith from one country or continent. Indeed, it has sometimes been described as the "original" belief system, because it shares numerous similarities with many shamanistic or earth-based religions from all corners of the globe.

ABOVE The mix of cultures and faiths that form the basis of the Wiccan faith brought about great changes in Europe not least the birth of the agricultural economy.

BELOW Stone circles were the churches and temples of the Wiccan faith and can still be found throughout Europe.

Over the centuries, increased trade between the tribes and peoples of Europe, combined with climatic change, famine, and occasional war (most notably the war between the Huns and the Roman Empire), caused a huge population shift from central to western Europe, which eventually resulted in intermingling of cultures and faiths. This exchange of knowledge and ideas also helped to change how people lived, with many of the hunter-gatherer tribes beginning to turn to farming as a means of providing themselves with food.

Farming must have at first seemed like a magical process to the hunter-gatherers, to whom an understanding of the seasons, and knowledge of where and when to plant crops or graze livestock, were all totally new. Among the tribes who introduced these new skills and ideas, farming was punctuated by magical and religious ceremonies.

Many of these ceremonies often included the occasional human sacrifice, evidence of which has been found across Europe in the form of well-preserved bodies discovered in peat bogs. These unfortunate individuals were not peasants, but usually high-ranking tribal members—possibly even the sons of tribal chiefs—ordinary peasants rarely being sacrificed because a bad season was regarded as a reflection of poor leadership. Because working with the land meant harnessing the power of Mother Nature, human sacrifice was seen as the ultimate offering that a tribe could make in order to appease the Goddess. Such instances of human sacrifice are examples of early democracy in action, and although its effects were rather more brutal than those of today, it is an interesting fact that a democratic system existed in ancient times.

Holding magical and religious ceremonies was thought to improve harvests and to encourage good weather to prevail in the seasons of the coming year. Some of these ceremonies still survive, and today form the basis of many of the festivals of the Wiccan, or witches', calendar (see pages 70 to 75). Even the Christian Church continues to celebrate many of the old pagan festivals, such as harvest thanksgiving and the mid-winter festival of Saturnalia (or, as Christians prefer to call it, Christmas).

ABOVE Pagan ceremonies marked important times in the farming year, and were believed to improve the weather in the following year!

BELOW The mid-winter festival of Christmas is just one of many much older Pagan festivals that has been adopted by the Christian faith.

RIGHT The use of herbs as a medicine is another skill that grew out of this mix of cultures, and it is now starting to grow in popularity as an alternative to modern drugs.

As a result of hunter-gatherer tribes taking up farming and no longer having to follow their food around, the peoples of Europe began to settle, and village-based communities started to take shape (see page 54). Together with the transition to an agricultural-based economy came the evolution of many other skills, such as those of healing and the practice of medicine. Smithcraft also played an important part in building these early communities, and was regarded as an almost magical skill whereby rocks could be turned into tools and weapons, while the blacksmith's forge was considered so valuable that it was often hidden outside the village to protect it from attack (see page 95).

In summary, although most modern Wiccans prefer to consider their practices to be Celtic or Druidic in origin, there is much evidence to suggest that Wicca is, in fact, a combination of cultures and faiths drawn from across Europe, and perhaps even from as far away as parts of Africa and Asia.

PAGANS, HEATHENS, WICCANS, AND WITCHES

Describing someone as a pagan, heathen, or witch is often taken to be an insult, although nothing could be further from the truth if you know what these words actually mean.

The word "pagan," which is frequently used to cover a wide range of non-mainstream spiritual beliefs, is derived from the Latin word *paganus*, meaning "fertile land," (it can also mean "rural" or a "villager/yokel") and was a name given by the Romans to the early farmers of Europe. It has been estimated that as many as one in twenty people today hold some kind of paganist belief.

The word "heathen" (again derived from Latin and meaning "heath-dweller") also formed part of the Roman vocabulary, and the name was later given to the Viking and Nordic tribes that settled in many parts of the British Isles. Even the original meanings of the words "Wiccan" and "witch", both Saxon in origin, were more complimentary than insulting, "Wiccan" meaning "to know" and "witch" meaning "wise" or "wise one". Indeed, it wasn't until the coming of Christianity that these words became derogatory terms that were used to turn the population against witchcraft and toward Christianity, part of a process that led to the persecution of witches by the Christian Church and to the burning time (see pages 18 to 22).

ABOVE The image of the forgiving Christ on the cross replaced the images of the older religions and brought about the first real decline in the Wiccan faith.

BELOW The Romans called Nordic tribes that settled in the heathland of Britain "Heathens" or "Heath dweller".

BIRTHS, BURIALS, AND BROOMSTICKS

During the hard, cruel times before healthcare and hospitals, child mortality rates were high, and even if one was lucky enough to survive into adulthood, life was still very tough. In an era when most people died before the age of forty, living into one's fifties or sixties was almost unheard of, and those people who did were often thought to be extremely wise ("witch", see above) and to possess the necessary skills or crafts of survival.

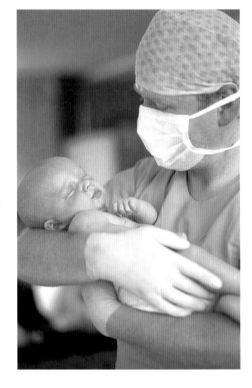

The term "crafty" (linked to the term "sly!") is often thought to be derogatory, but if you think of the crafty old fox, who uses his cunning of craftiness in order to survive, it begins to take on a less sinister meaning.

Although frequently uneducated, such "old witches" were practitioners of the old ways and cared for the sick, tending to everything from pulling teeth to delivering babies. The local witch was a healer, a midwife, an agony aunt, a social worker, and even a matchmaker.

The function of identifying the right people for marriage was extremely important because it helped to strengthen the witch's village, pairing up couples from different communities, for example, in many cases forging links and preventing conflict between potentially rival villages. Witches would often meet up, normally at one of the pagan or Wiccan festivals, to discuss how best to help and care for the people of their villages, as well as trying to keep the peace between them, all of which constituted much of the coven's work.

RIGHT Before modern-day medicine the witches were the doctors and midwives.

BELOW The fox symbolizes the use of the skills or crafts of survival and, like the Wiccan faith, it was also vilified by the newer religions.

The marriage ceremony was often performed by the local witch, too, either by "hand-fasting", or tying the couple's hands together to symbolize their union, or by having them jump over a broomstick. (The term "living over the broom" is still used in many parts of Britain to describe a couple who are living together, but are not legally married.) In some parts of Europe, the local blacksmith performed the marriage ceremony over his anvil, demonstrating another link between witches and blacksmiths, both groups of people being seen as having supernatural powers.

Among the many supernatural skills attributed to witches is the ability to call up the spirits of people who have recently died, a practice that is called necromancy. In the Old Testament (1 Samuel 28), for example, it is said that King Saul approached one of the witches of Endor in the hope of raising the spirit of his advisor, Samuel, so that Saul could consult him about his coming battle against the Philistines. The spirit of Samuel was so enraged by being raised from the dead, however, that he told the king (who had banned the practice) that because the king had broken his own law against witchcraft he would lose the battle against the Philistines, which he did.

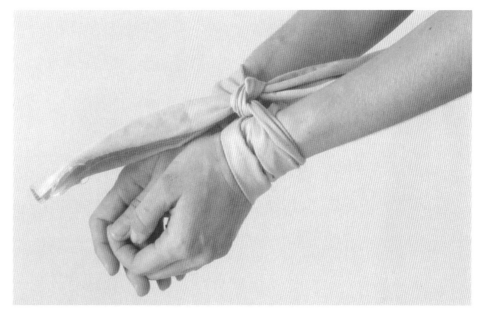

ABOVE *The marriage ceremony would also be performed by the witch, either by means of hand fasting, or by getting the happy couple to jump over a broom.*

BELOW *Witches were attributed with the supernatural power of necromancy, the ability to the summon the spirits of those who have passed on.*

One of the most famous practitioners of necromancy was the notorious Edward Kelly, an associate of the famous magician Dr. John Dee, astrologer royal to Queen Elizabeth I of England. Kelly, who was reputed to have raised the spirits of the dead for his own foul purposes on a number of occasions, was known as the "crop-eared rogue", the cropping of ears being a punishment for stealing, or other types of crime, in sixteenth-century England, which gives an indication of the kind of person he was. Kelly came to a sticky end while on a spying mission to Germany in 1582. Whether this was retribution for having disturbed the spirits of the dead, who can say, but then again, who knows?

Although I do not encourage the practice of necromancy, communion with the dead has formed an important part of pagan and shamanistic ceremonies for many thousands of years and should therefore be looked at in a wider context. Many Native American teachings, for instance, speak of the fireside council (or counsel) of the ancestors, whereby

ABOVE Dealings with the spirits of the dead is possible, but not encouraged.

RIGHT The native American shaman were often called upon to seek the wise counsel of the tribe's long-dead ancestors.

a shaman seeks the wisdom of past generations of the tribe in order to help the present tribal members along their path through life. Yet, while there are a number of similar shamanistic ceremonies from other parts of the world that can be regarded in a similarly positive light, their practice has only served to further the persecution and misunderstanding of witchcraft.

The burning time

As the Christian faith spread westward, the fear and persecution of witches reached almost hysterical proportions, leading to what is now referred to as the "burning time" (although most suspected witches were actually hanged for their imagined crimes). It was the burning time that brought about the first real decline in the age-old practise of witchcraft.

The Christian Church did much to condemn and vilify witches and followers of the old ways, but it wasn't until the reign of James VI of Scotland (later James I of England) that the persecution started to take a more sinister turn. While King James was traveling to Denmark to find a bride, he was caught up in a terrible storm at sea and immediately blamed the witches of his native Scotland, accusing them of trying to prevent his marriage. John Fian, a schoolmaster from Saltpans, near Edinburgh, was the chief suspect and, after being cruelly tortured, was burned at the stake for supposedly raising the storm. King James then went on to publish a book entitled *The Discouverie of Witchcraft* ("Discouverie" being the old English spelling of "Discovery"), a sort of "how to find a witch" or "which witch manual" of its time. This inaccurate and misleading book led to hundreds, if not thousands, of innocent people being put to death.

King James is also famous for authorizing the rewriting of the Christian Bible, and the King James Bible that still forms the basis of Christian worship in the Church of England contains a number of pieces of anti-witch propaganda. In this version of the Bible's book of Deuteronomy, for instance, it is stated that "Thou shalt not consult astrologers or

BELOW The King James version of the Christian Bible contains a number of mis-translations that were used to condemn witchcraft.

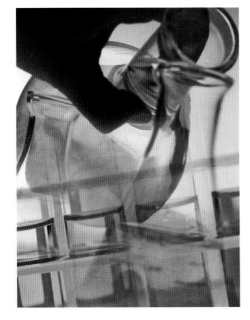

soothsayers," the text later goes on to say, "Thou shalt not suffer a witch to live." In this instance, the word "witch" is a mistranslation of the Greek text. The correct translation is "poisoner," but as a result of the witch's knowledge of herbs, the words "witch" and "poisoner" became synonymous.

It seems that the "Great Bard," William Shakespeare, was compelled to write *Macbeth* (1605), also known as "The Scottish Play," in order to please King James (by then king of England), for it not only portrayed witches in a bad light, but also praised the king's own

RIGHT The "Great Bard" William Shakespeare wrote about witchcraft in a number of his plays.

ancestors, the Banquo family. This traditionally unlucky play was not the only one that Shakespeare wrote on the subject of witchcraft and the occult, however: *A Midsummer Night's Dream* (1595) is full of references to magic and folklore, as are *The Tempest* (1611),

ABOVE The witches' understanding of herbal medicine led to them being accused of being little more than poisoners of the innocent.

Love's Labour's Lost (1594), *The Winter's Tale* (1610) and *The Merchant of Venice* (1596).

During the burning time, one could be accused of being a witch for almost anything — from being old or unmarried to keeping a pet (or familiar)- a practice that was not that common in seventeenth-century England, when most animals were kept as livestock, beasts of burden, or for hunting. Most witches were healers who lived close to nature and apart from the general population, and they would often take in and care for sick and injured animals however.

Although keeping almost any animal could lead to one being accused of being a witch, first and foremost among the suspect animals were cats, followed by birds (especially owls and crows), toads and frogs, weasels, and any type of large, wolf-like dog. As a result of keeping pets, these poor, old, unfortunate folk, who did no one any harm, and in most cases tried to help and cure their community's sick people, were rounded up and put on trial, in most cases a foregone conclusion that ended in the alleged witch being put to death.

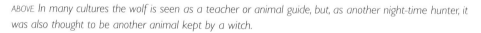

ABOVE In many cultures the wolf is seen as a teacher or animal guide, but, as another night-time hunter, it was also thought to be another animal kept by a witch.

ABOVE The wise winged hunter of the night, the owl, has often been associated with witches.

Not all witches were peasants, however, one of the most famous of all witches to be put to death being Elena Cobham, the Duchess of Gloucester, who was not only a woman of title, but also the aunt of King Henry VI of England, and was implicated in an attempt to poison her nephew. Nor did the Duchess of Gloucester represent the only link between witchcraft and the aristocracy. The Plantagenet dynasty (which took its name from the Latin words *planta* and *genista*, "sprig" and "broom"), whose members ruled England from 1154 to 1485, for instance, is suspected to have had a very long association with the Wiccan faith.

The coming of the Great Plague went hand in hand with the increased persecution of alleged witches, the seventeenth-century population of England regarding the outbreak of the plague as a divine curse sent by God to punish the evils in their society. With the finger of blame once again being pointed at witchcraft, those people who thought that they might be suspected of being witches fled, for fear of being burnt at the stake. Yet, by their flight they not only unwittingly spread the plague, but also deprived their home communities of the nearest thing that they had to a doctor, in turn leading to many more deaths.

The witch-hunts continued with the trial of the witches of Pendle and the execution of many so-called "witches", of which the most famous was Alice Nutter, a poor, and somewhat simple-minded, woman, who sadly gave her name to yet another derogatory term: "a nutter", meaning a mad person.

In East Anglia, Matthew Hopkins, a Puritan who held the infamous and self-appointed title

ABOVE Originally it was thought that a witch could only be killed by burning, but with firewood often in short supply, most had to be hanged due to the cost of lumber.

"witchfinder general", oversaw the trials of many hundreds of alleged witches, hanging sixty in Essex in one year alone. Hopkins would charge the local authorities for his services, and they frequently also had to pay for his lodgings while he was in the area hunting down witches, as well as for

ABOVE. The followers of the Jewish faith faced similar persecution, this being yet another of the older religions that was nearly wiped out.

accommodation for his staff, which included at least one executioner, who also presented a bill to the local authorities for services rendered. It could therefore be argued that Hopkins' motives had more to do with profit than with moral or religious conviction. Hopkins was eventually challenged and subjected to one of his own witch-finding tests. The test was simple: if a suspect was thrown into a river and drowned, he or she was innocent, if the suspect floated, then he or she was deemed a witch. The evil and sadistic Hopkins failed the test and was accordingly put to death.

The persecution of witches and adherents to the Wiccan faith can be compared with Hitler's persecution of the Jews during the 1930s and 1940s in terms of its hysteria. Much of this hysteria is now thought to have stemmed from ergot poisoning, ergot being a mold-like fungus that, during wet summers, grows on rye, which, in seventeenth-century Europe was used in place of wheat to make bread. Once the rye bread had been ingested, the ergot would cause severe stomach cramps, hallucinations and, in most cases, a very painful death. As their families looked on in horror, victims of ergot poisoning would writhe in agony, seeing all the demons and horrors of hell coming at them out of the walls and floors, for which witchcraft was immediately blamed. Although I suspect that many witches knew of ergot (probably referring to it by another name) and were aware of what it could do, I am equally sure that almost all of the cases of ergot poisoning were accidental. Ergot poisoning occurred in many parts of mainland Europe and, along with cases of rabies, added to the hysteria that witchcraft aroused in the general population. Both rabies and ergot poisoning are also thought to have fueled many of the legends of vampires and werewolves.

The last witchcraft trial in Britain was that of Helen Duncan, which took place in Portsmouth in 1944. Having been accused of witchcraft, after receiving a vision of the sinking of the Royal Navy cruiser Burnham, which was classified information, Helen Duncan was found guilty, but was at least spared the death sentence — instead being imprisoned.

The last witch-burning took place in Ireland in 1902, the sentence of death by burning was passed not by a court, but by an angry mob of private citizens who murdered an unfortunate woman for some imagined crime.

ABOVE *When the summers were particularly wet, a mold-like fungus would grow on the rye—when this was used to make bread it lead to ergot poisoning.*

THE SURVIVAL OF THE WICCAN FAITH

Despite the persecution and mistrust of witches and followers of occult practices, interest in, and study of, these subjects have continued, often in secret. Many organizations, such as the Hermetic Order of the Golden Dawn and, according to some, even the Freemasons, perpetuated the ancient, and supposedly forgotten, practices of the past. During the eighteenth and nineteenth centuries, many such secret organizations sprang up, which, although they were well hidden from the mainstream population, helped to preserve the old ways and to ensure their survival to this day.

The 1920s saw a more public renewal of interest in the occult that in turn eventually led to a revival of the practices of witchcraft under the leadership of people like Aleister Crowley, who, despite once having been called "the most evil man in Britain", was considered by many to have been a visionary who was well ahead of his time. Although some of his admirers were the followers of his own branch of magic—"Crowleyanity", as he called it—it must be said that he was a brave and clever man who wrote a number of groundbreaking books on the subjects of the occult and Wicca. Crowley made some wild statements during his lifetime, including the claim that he was the "Great Beast" (666), as well as the reincarnation of Edward Kelly (see page 16), such outrageous statements were most likely due to his drug addictions, addictions that in the end contributed to his death in 1947. Despite the controversy that surrounded him, Crowley should be remembered for his groundbreaking research and pioneering spirit.

Finally, the name that stands out above all in the annals of the Wiccan faith is that of Margaret Murray, whose extensive research and books on Wicca, such as *The God of the Witches*, have shaped the Wiccan faith as we know it today, causing some to give her the title the "Mother of Modern-day Wicca". No one has contributed more than Margaret Murray to the revival of Wiccan witchcraft.

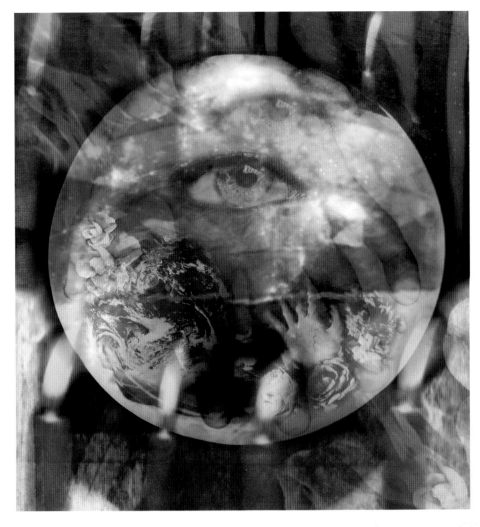

CHAPTER I

HOCUS-POCUS

The use of spells is synonymous with witchcraft, but what exactly is a spell? How does a spell work, and how can spells be relevant to us today in our daily lives?

First and foremost, you will need to understand the way in which a spell is cast, and the effect that it can have on the world around you. The principles behind Wiccan magic will be discussed in more detail later, after we've discovered what a spell actually is.

WHAT IS A SPELL?

The word "spell" originates from a variety of sources: the Saxon word *spel*, which means "a saying" or "a story"; the Icelandic word *spjal*, which also means "a saying" or "a spoken word"; and the Gothic word *spill*, which means "fable" (a type of story or narrative). In the English language, to spell something is to set out a group of letters in the correct manner to create a word. This is, in some ways, similar to casting a magical spell, but, instead of writing it out on paper, the spell is written in thought and is acted upon with the intention of bringing about a set of circumstances in order to achieve a desired goal.

BELOW When you write you spell out words with pen and paper, but when you use magic you spell out what you want to achieve, with thought and intent.

Spells normally fall into one of the following four categories.

Protective

1

A protective spell protects a person

(or dwelling) from harm or danger. It is

usually used to protect the

person who casts it,

but can also protect

someone else,

such as a friend

or family member.

A curse or taboo

2

Casting a curse or taboo is a way of directing

bad luck or danger toward someone else,

which can often be very dangerous and goes

against the ethics of spell-casting (see page 31).

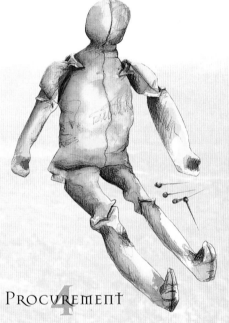

Transformation

3

A transformation spell can be used to change

the appearance of an object, animal or person,

be it the appearance of the person who casts

the spell or of someone else.

Procurement

4

A procurement spell normally has some

desired goal, such as to cleanse, cure or

encourage love, or to procure a material

item, like a new car.

The longest part of any spell is often the planning stage: working out exactly what you want and how to achieve it can take weeks, or even months, depending on the spell.

The actual power that a spell exerts once it has been cast can only help to take you along a particular path or toward a certain set of events. If you're not prepared to work toward achieving your goal in a practical and physical way as well, the spell will often fail. For instance, if you cast a love spell, but never go out afterward, how can you realistically expect to meet your true love?

Most of us understand the principle of positive thought, that is, the practice of setting a goal and remaining focused on it until it has been achieved. In this way, anything from deciding that you want a vacation, a new apartment, or even a new partner, can be said to be a type of spell. As with positive thought, a spell is merely an attitude of mind. It is said that faith can move mountains (although I personally believe that a digger and a fleet of trucks would be of more use), and if you really believe in yourself, you can do almost anything.

HOW DO SPELLS WORK?

We are all familiar with the stereotypical image of the witch, normally dressed in black and wearing a pointed hat, chanting a spell over a cauldron while she stirs a bubbling potion. This view of witches arose from their persecution and demonization by the Christian Church (see pages 18 to 22), folklore, and Hollywood, and is far removed from the spell-casting of Wiccan witchcraft.

Because a spell involves the use of thought, we first need to look at the human mind and how it works. Many people believe that we exist on a number of levels of reality, and in most occult philosophical systems there are thought to be five (although some of these can be subdivided, making a total of eight).

ABOVE Cauldrons are another item linked to witches and spell casting, though they were a valuable item for herbal remedies, most spells don't really require the use of these rather large cooking utensils.

THE PHYSICAL LEVEL

This is the lowest level of existence, where our physical bodies and minds exist, the world in which we spend every waking moment. At this level we perceive everything through our five terrestrial senses: sight, smell, hearing, touch, and taste. This level can be symbolized by the Earth.

RIGHT Linked closely with our sense of taste, our sense of smell is subtle and delicate. Though not always obvious, it is our ability to sense animal pheromones that controls human attraction and interaction.

BELOW RIGHT Although often considered one of the less important of our physical senses, the ability to sense things by touch is vital to maintaining our sense of reality and keeping ourselves grounded.

BELOW LEFT The physical-level existence is symbolized by the planet Earth, our home world, and the only planet in the known universe so far to be able to physically support human life.

The etheric level 2

This level is made up of an energy, ether, that I can only describe as "near matter". People working in certain areas of science believe that they have discovered this energy source, which they call "dark matter", a substance that is believed to exist all around us and is thought to form the building blocks of all physical matter. This level is symbolized by the moon.

ABOVE The etheric level is represented by the moon and just as the moon effects the tides on earth the etheric level effects the physical world.

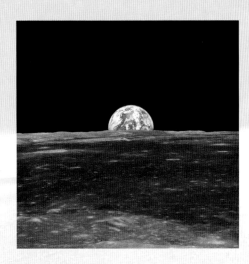

The astral (upper and lower) level 3

Mars the masculine and fiery planet of war.

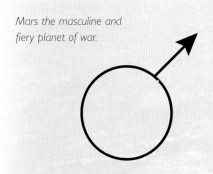

Venus the female and emotional planet of love.

The lower astral level is governed by our instincts and passions, while the upper astral level is ruled by our emotions. The astral level is where we feel our desires and attraction to people or objects, as well as our urge to relate to others on a higher, non-physical level. The lower astral level is symbolized by the planet Mars and the upper astral level by the planet Venus.

BELOW Emotions rule all our lives, and although totally irrational, they form an important part of our thought process.

The mental (upper and lower) level

At this level our minds start to explore the personal and individual. The lower mental level analyzes concepts and ideas and deals with the accumulation of memories. The upper mental level deals with higher, spiritual and non-rational thought, such as faith and spiritual belief. The lower mental level is symbolized by the planet Saturn and the upper mental level by the planet Mercury.

ABOVE *Faith and religious belief is one thing that sets us apart from all other animals, the expectance of higher powers (or gods) forms the basis of every civilization and culture throughout history.*

ABOVE *The planet Saturn symbolizes organization, structure, and time, while Mercury represents messages and communication with higher powers.*

The spiritual (upper and lower) level

This is the highest of all levels. The lower spiritual level is where the individuality of the soul is set, defining the part of our personalities that survives physical death. The higher spiritual level is where our minds connect directly with the divine creative force. It is at this level that the concept of self is replaced by the concept of unity with all things. The lower spiritual level is symbolized by the planet Jupiter and the higher spiritual level by the sun.

ABOVE *Jupiter and the sun represents the individual soul joining with the ultimate source all existence.*

When you cast a spell, all that you are doing is focusing on a thought or intention until it becomes implanted in your higher consciousness, thereby effecting changes on the etheric level and beyond. (Although elementary magic only works on the first two levels, the physical and etheric—the elements are thought to exist only on these two levels—it is still important to understand how our minds work.) According to the theory of reincarnation, our higher levels of consciousness are immortal, surviving physical death to live out other lives.

BELOW In the theory of reincarnation, higher levels of the human mind are thought to survive physical death to live out other lives.

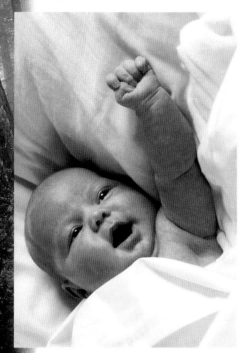

ABOVE Death comes to take us all but it is not the end—as with all things, life goes on, and as one generation ends, a new one is born.

THE ETHICS OF SPELLS AND SPELL-CASTING

AT THIS POINT I WOULD LIKE TO GIVE A FEW WORDS OF WARNING ABOUT THE ETHICS OF SPELLS AND SPELL-CASTING. WHATEVER YOUR INTENT BEHIND A SPELL, IT WILL ALWAYS COME BACK IN THREE WAYS AND AT THREE LEVELS, BUT IF YOU FOLLOW THESE FIVE SIMPLE RULES, YOU SHOULDN'T HAVE ANY TROUBLE.

1. DON'T EVER CAST A SPELL IF YOUR INTENT IS TO CAUSE HARM IN ANY WAY, SHAPE, OR FORM.

2. DON'T CAST A SPELL TO MANIPULATE ANYONE AGAINST THEIR WILL OR THEIR NATURAL COURSE OF FATE. FATE IS A VERY POWERFUL FORCE, AND, NO MATTER HOW GOOD YOU THINK YOU ARE AT SPELL-CASTING, FATE WILL ALWAYS WIN (I KNOW THIS FROM BITTER EXPERIENCE!)

3. DON'T EVER ASSUME ANYTHING. EVEN THOUGH YOU MAY THINK THAT YOU KNOW EVERYTHING THAT THERE IS TO KNOW ABOUT A PERSON OR SITUATION, YOU PROBABLY DON'T. FEW OF US KNOW EVERYTHING ABOUT OURSELVES, SO THINK CAREFULLY ABOUT WHAT YOU INTEND TO DO BEFORE CASTING A SPELL.

4. DON'T EVER CAST A SPELL FOR YOUR OWN PERSONAL GAIN IF THAT WILL IN TURN BRING BAD LUCK OR LOSS TO ANOTHER PERSON.

5. BE VERY CAREFUL HOW YOU WORD A SPELL WHEN YOU ARE CASTING IT. REMEMBER THAT IF IT WORKS, YOU WILL GET EXACTLY WHAT YOU ASKED FOR, AND THAT IF YOU WORD IT INCORRECTLY, YOU COULD END UP BREAKING ONE OF THE OTHER RULES.

I KNOW THAT THEY MAY SEEM RATHER CONFUSING, BUT IF YOU TAKE A LITTLE TIME TO THINK THEM THROUGH, YOU WILL SEE THAT THESE RULES ON ETHICS MAKE SENSE, AS WELL AS BEING FAIRLY EASY TO FOLLOW.

THE SPELL-CASTING CEREMONY

The magical ceremonies associated with spell-casting are often viewed with suspicion and fear, with sinister images of stone circles and black-robed figures making incantations under the full moon often springing to mind. Yet, while many witches still take part in such ceremonies, most spell-casting doesn't require any dramatic locations or costumes.

All that you need is a little floor space, about 3 or 4 feet in diameter, and some peace and quiet. If you have to rearrange your home a little, then all the better, because this can make spell-casting feel like a bit of a ritual, adding to its ceremonial nature.

Because the space that you use for spell-casting must be sacred in your mind, spend a little time clearing and preparing your designated area. This is a good way of psyching up your higher mind, preparing it for the ceremony

There are many different ways of casting a spell, but, while the names or words used may vary greatly, the fundamental details remain unchanged. Providing that you understand and follow these details, you can adapt the ceremony to whatever you feel most comfortable with. Remember that it's not just what you say, it's what you feel that's important, and that the words or tools that you use are simply a means of helping you to attain the right feeling.

ABOVE It is important to have the right amount of space for a spell-casting ceremony, this need not be a huge area, a few feet of floor space will do.

BELOW The vast stone circles of the past were used for magic ceremonies by the Wiccan faith, for your ceremony you will need to create your own personal stone circle.

Spend some time thinking about the ceremony and about what you want your spell to achieve. Consider what it is that you want to change about yourself or your life, and then think about how that change will make you feel. Hold the feeling in your mind as you try to find a single word that describes it, a word that you can use in the ceremony to trigger it.

Before performing the ceremony, you could take a bath or meditate. It is also helpful to wear clothes in which you feel comfortable (although some witches believe that you should be totally naked when casting a spell, this isn't compulsory). Once you've completed your preparations and feel relaxed and focused, you are ready to begin,

ABOVE You need to be relaxed but focused for a spell-casting ceremony.

RIGHT You may find a hot bath helps you to attain the right atmosphere of relaxation.

BELOW Meditation exercises are extremely useful, not just for spell casting but for relaxation and stress relief.

A basic spell-casting ceremony

The best ceremony for casting a spell is normally one that you have worked out for yourself, but you can only do this properly if you have grasped the basic concepts. The following ceremony is a basic example, and although it can be quite effective, it may not work for everyone.

Setting out a circle

The first thing that you need to do is to set out a circle. You will need just enough space to enable you to sit and move around within it. Depending on the tools (if any) that you will be using, the circle needs to be only a few feet in diameter. Set out the circle by placing four stones, candles, or elementary tools (see page 34) at each of the four points of the compass. (I recommend that you use a compass to determine the four points because any error could make the spell ineffective.)

Because the space that you use for spell-casting must be sacred in your mind, spend a little time clearing and preparing your designated area. This is a good way of psyching up your higher mind, preparing it for the ceremony.

ABOVE You may find it useful to have representations of the four elements within your circle.

Setting up a ring of protection

The next part of any spell-casting ceremony, the setting up of a ring of protection, is very important. Because you will be working with your higher consciousness, you will need to encircle yourself in a ring of protection to

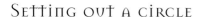

ABOVE When you physically set up protection (i.e, setting out stones or walking around the circle) you need to move clockwise, but when you do it using pure mental visualization (i.e, imagining a protective wall) you move counter-clockwise.

keep your higher mind safe from any negative forces. I have come across various ways of protecting yourself while spell-casting over the years, but there are three that always come to mind, as follows.

I Walk around the circle counter-clockwise, three times for the upper hemisphere ("As is above") and three times for the lower hemisphere ("So is below"). While you are walking around the circle the first three times, imagine yourself moving upward from the surface of the Earth until you can touch the moon. While you are walking around the circle for the last three times, imagine yourself moving downward through the Earth until you can touch its core.

2 The next step is to lay out eight stones, each representing one of the fire or solar festivals of the Wiccan calendar (see pages 70 to 75). Starting in the south-east and moving counter-clockwise, state which festival it represents as you place each stone in position (saying, for example, "I place this stone in honor of the time of Beltane.") When you position the last stone in the east, finish off by saying, "I place this stone in honor of the spring equinox and close this circle of protection around me."

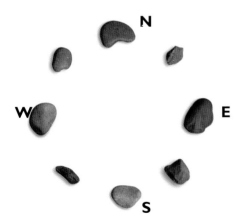

ABOVE When setting out the circle (whatever number of stones you are using), try and use four larger stones for the main points of the compass.

You can also use twelve stones representing either each of the twelve signs of the zodiac or the twelve months of the year, whatever makes you feel more comfortable.

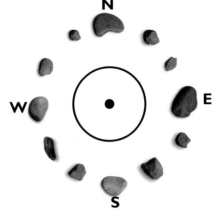

ABOVE If you are using twelve stones to represent the twelve signs of the zodiac you could try starting with the sign you were born under (or the month you were born in) and moving clockwise until you've built your circle.

The setting-out of a stone circle is a very old practice, and although many of the stone circles of the past were much larger and more permanent, setting out your own, smaller circle can be very effective. It can also provide you with a safe and sacred space in which to meditate. A friend of mine once asked me to help him with meditation, so I showed him how to set out his own, personal circle based on the signs of the zodiac. Although he doesn't use the circle for spell-casting, he finds the setting-out ceremony a useful trigger for relaxing his mind in preparation for meditation.

3 The next method of protection is not so much the best, but the most adaptable, because it can be used at any time to protect yourself against negativity or psychic attack. All that you need to do is to imagine a blue, fiery wall moving counter-clockwise around you. You may have to practice this a few times while meditating, but once you have mastered it you will find it an extremely effective form of defense. A fellow-witch friend of mine sometimes calls this the "shields-up" method; a Star Trek fan, he imagines himself to be a starship captain on the bridge of a federation starship, and whenever he feels danger he says "Shields up!" and envisages being protected by a wall of blue flame.

ABOVE Meditation can help you to visualize the intent or desire of your spell.

HONORING THE COMPASS POINTS

Once you have protected yourself, you will need to honor the four points of the compass and their associated elements by bowing to them, starting with the east and moving clockwise until you finish with the north.

ABOVE Once you've set protection you'll need to bow to (or honor) the four points of the compass.

For each of the four points of the compass, you will need to select a trinity of items, or three things, that tie the compass point's direction with an element and gender, as follows.

I Direction. Choose something that represents the direction, perhaps a place, a country, a city, or even a religion or culture.

Remember to think about and try and visualize the direction you are bowing to, this can be a place, city or country.

2 Element. Choose something that both represents the element of the direction and ties in with whatever it was that you chose to symbolize the direction.

BELOW You also need to find something that links the direction to the element it represents (i.e. earth, fire, water or air), visualization tools can be useful to help you with this.

3 Gender. Choose something (perhaps a person) that is either male or female and also ties in with what you chose to represent—either the direction or the element or both. Note that the east and south are regarded as masculine, and the west and north as feminine.

ABOVE Cultures and civilizations can help you visualize a particular direction, Egypt is one of many civilizations that could be used for the east.

To clarify, I'll now give an example for the north. If you live in the US, Alaska could represent the northerly direction, in which case you would say, "I bow to the power of the north. I think of the north, I think of Alaska." The next step is to think of the element, which, in the case of the north, is earth, so, tying in what you said about the direction, you would say, "I bow to the power of the north. I think of the north, I think of Alaska. I think of the smell of the earth out there on the tundra." Now you have to identify the gender of the north, which is female. Tying in the direction and element, you would say, "I bow to the power of the north. I think of the north, I think of Alaska. I think of the smell of the earth out there on the tundra. I think of how the harsh beauty of the tundra reminds me of the beauty of Mother Nature."

LEFT Finally you need to find something that also ties in the gender associated to the direction and element, this could be a statue of a person of mythical figure linked to that direction or element.

ABOVE The snowy terrain of Alaska can be used to help you to visualize the direction of the north.

Always try to visualize what you are saying, and remember that it isn't a race, so you don't have to rush the process, and can take as long as you need. Focus on the trinity: direction, element and gender.

Empowering your tools

If you intend to use any tools when casting your spell, you should now empower them. Tools that you could use include cards (see page 60, 61), candles (see page 60), a photograph or any item that will help you to visualize the intent of the spell.

Because three is a magic number (or a trinity, and think how

many trinities are part of religious belief, such as Christianity's father, son, and holy spirit), try to use three items if you can. When you are more proficient at spell-casting and understand the principles of magic better, you may want to experiment with different numbers: instead of using three tools, you could use seven, or four, for example, depending on the purpose or intent of your spell (See Ways of Wicca, pages 44 to 67). While you are new to spell-casting, however, it's best start with three if possible.

To empower your tools, take each of them in turn and once again bow to each of the four points (directions) of the compass, as you did before when

honoring the compass points (remember to use the trinity), and start in the east and move clockwise until you finish in the north.

What you do next depends on the spell or what type of tools (if any) you are using, these could be cards (page 60, 61), candles (page 60) or fith-faths (pages 61 to 62).

LEFT AND ABOVE Visualization tools could be anything from a set or divination cards to a photo, all tools do is help you to see what you want to achieve.

VISUALIZING, CASTING, AND CLOSING THE SPELL

The next step is to visualize the intent of the spell. As you are visualizing it, feel the force of your will growing within you. Let it build for as long as you can and then, just before you feel it start to reach its peak, hold its power and state the intent of the spell.

ABOVE You may want to practice visualizing the intent of the spell a few times while meditating, before you attempt a spell-casting ceremony.

To release its power, all that you have to do is to imagine pushing the force and intent of the spell upward, onto the etheric level.

After this, bow to and thank the powers of either of the four quarters or, if you have worked with them, the four elemental lords whom you will need to banish by reversing the sign of the pentacle that you called them with (see page 41) starting in the east and finishing in the north.

A SUMMARY OF SPELL-CASTING

LET'S RUN THOUGHT THE BASIC SPELL-CASTING CEREMONY AGAIN.

1 Set out the circle by placing four stones, candles, or items that symbolize the four directions (remember to check them with a compass) in position.

2 Set up a ring of protection around yourself using any of the three methods described above. Always remember to protect yourself.

3 Now either call the elemental lords or bow to the four points of the compass, starting with the east, then turning to the south, then to the west, and finally to the north.

4 If you are using tools for visualization, take each in turn and bow to the four points of the compass, remembering the trinity of direction, element, and gender. Start with the east and move clockwise until you finish with the north.

5 Now visualize the intent of the spell, let the force of your will build, and then release it by stating what you want the spell to achieve.

6 Close the spell by bowing and thanking the four quarters.

HIGH AND LOW MAGIC

In occult theory there are generally considered to be two forms of magic: high magic and low magic. Low magic is an individual form of magic that uses one's own, personal power based on one's faith and cultural beliefs. Although low magic is not as powerful as high magic, it is both more adaptable and safer. High magic, on the other hand, taps into the power source of the great manifest or divine creative force (depending on which terminology you prefer).

The ceremonies used to invoke high magic are often very long and complex, and are based on the ancient teachings of a number of long-dead civilizations.

Because high magic uses the ultimate divine source, it is extremely powerful, but any mistakes can have serious consequences. It's important to understand that this divine power goes beyond any ethical constraints and is neither good nor evil—it just is. A friend of mine describes it in terms of filling a bath with water: "You can fill a bath with water to bathe a baby or to drown a baby; the water doesn't care either way."

To explain the difference between the two forms of magic further, I shall use the Native American idea of the life-walk, the path that we have to take in life. Our lives follow this life-walk, and although we may wander off it occasionally, we always find our way back to the path that we are fated to walk in our lives. If we live our lives without using magic, we walk along the path, taking each day as it comes. Although this slow pace can be boring at times, it is safe.

ABOVE Many cultures believe that we all walk a pre-destined path in life

BELOW Our life walk may be slow and boring, but we always get to where we need to be in life, even if it takes a while.

ABOVE Even the more established religions practice high and low magic, the Christian faiths are sometimes divided into high and low church.

LEFT Concepts of good and evil exist in every culture and religion, but the true nature of the divine power goes beyond such basic principles.

When you use low magic, your pace speeds up a little, as though you were riding a bicycle, which helps you to travel faster, but still relies on your power to propel it. Although you are traveling a little quicker, if something goes wrong it may hurt a bit, but won't cause any lasting harm, just like falling off a bike.

Using high magic is like jumping into a high-performance racing car: you will travel a lot faster, but if you can't drive, the likelihood of having an accident is very high, and, when you are traveling at high speeds, accidents can be very serious.

ABOVE Using low magic is like riding a bike, it speeds things up but you are still using your own power to propel yourself along your life walk.

BELOW High magic requires skill and practice—just like driving a sports car, it's faster than walking, but if you don't know what you are doing it can have dangerous consequences.

Using the elemental lords

Most things have gray areas, and high and low magic are no exceptions, the gray area in this instance being the use of the elemental lords. To continue with the transport analogy, using the elemental lords is like driving a small automatic car along the life-walk. It is relatively easy to drive, travels a little faster than a bicycle, and if you do have an accident along the way, it may shake you up a bit, or even hurt you slightly, but you will survive, and will almost certainly be able to walk away from the scene of the accident.

ABOVE Using the elemental lords can be compared to driving a small automatic car—it uses another power to propel you along, but it is at a relatively safe and controllable speed.

Just as each element is linked with a point of the compass, so it is also linked with an elemental lord (see pages 46 to 48). When you are casting a spell, you can call or invoke the elemental lords to boost the power of the spell (although you won't usually need any extra power when casting most spells).

When summoning the elemental lords, instead of bowing to the powers of the four points of the compass—the elements—you should bow to the lords that control the elements, and call them by name (right). Starting with the east and moving clockwise until you finish with the north, each time that you call an elemental lord you will need to make the sign of the pentagram, starting with the point of the pentagram that corresponds to the particular elemental lord that you are invoking (see right).

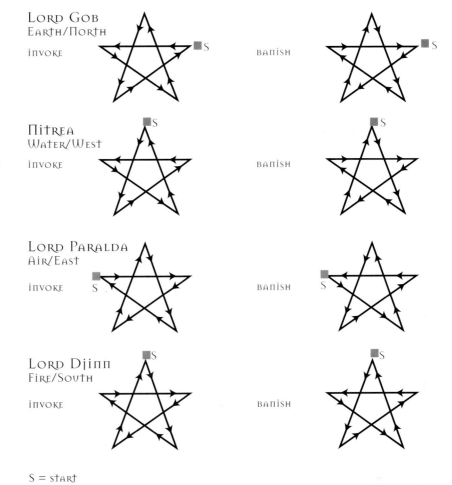

LORD GOB
EARTH/NORTH
INVOKE   BANISH

NITREA
WATER/WEST
INVOKE   BANISH

LORD PARALDA
AIR/EAST
INVOKE   BANISH

LORD DJINN
FIRE/SOUTH
INVOKE   BANISH

S = start

AFTER YOU HAVE MADE THE SIGN WITH YOUR INDEX FINGER, SAY, "I INVOKE THEE, O LORD [state the lord's name], LORD OF [state the element], ELEMENT OF THE [state the direction]."

WHEN YOU HAVE FINISHED YOUR SPELL, YOU WILL NEED TO BANISH EACH ELEMENTAL LORD IN TURN BY REVERSING THE SIGN OF THE PENTAGRAM THAT YOU USED TO INVOKE EACH WITH, SAYING, "I BANISH THEE, O LORD [state the lord's name], LORD OF [state the element], ELEMENT OF THE [state the direction]." FINALLY, BOW AND THANK THE ELEMENTAL LORD.

REMEMBER THAT YOU DON'T ALWAYS NEED TO USE THE ELEMENTAL LORDS' POWERS, BUT IF YOU DO, MAKE SURE THAT IT'S FOR A GOOD REASON, FOR IN MAGIC, JUST AS IN EVERYDAY LIFE, IT IS CONSIDERED RUDE TO BOTHER SOMEONE FOR NO REASON.

A few final words

When they think of witchcraft and spell-casting, most people probably conjure up the image of a curse being pronounced. Although a curse can be described as a type of spell, it is an extremely dangerous form of magic, which, in my experience, often does more harm to the person who casts it than to the intended victim.

The simple rule to remember when casting any spell is that whatever you send out will come back to you. According to an old belief, bad luck comes in threes, and if you cast a spell and send out bad intent, it will always come back to you in three ways or on three levels, so it would be better not to do it! If someone is intent on causing you harm, because they will normally fall foul of themselves, you won't need to curse them. A protection spell will usually be sufficient, and if you follow the rules on the ethics of spell-casting (see page 31), you shouldn't have much to worry about. If, on the other hand, you cast a spell with good intent, especially one that helps someone else, it will again come back to you in three ways and on three levels, but in this case all of them will be good.

ABOVE *Whatever your intent or desire magic should (like all skills in life) be used to help others and not to hinder them!*

When planning and casting any type of spell, try to keep it as simple as possible. This is because a spell can sometimes have a dramatic effect on the world around you, and if it is too complex, you may inadvertently alter your life.

In the Wiccan faith there is one rule that, if broken, in turn breaks the power of a spell: as soon as you have decided to cast a spell, and even after you have cast it, you must always

ABOVE The most important rule of all is the rule of silence, one you have cast a spell you must keep it to yourself, to tell someone will only break the power of the spell.

keep it to yourself. Say nothing to anyone, otherwise the spell will be ineffective.

Finally, try to keep your spell-casting to a minimum. Life can be complicated enough without a barrage of spells bouncing around (and you may want to keep a record of the spells you have cast to help you to avoid casting two contradictory spells).

THE BOOK OF SHADOWS

TRADITIONALLY, THE BOOK OF SHADOWS IS A PERSONAL HANDBOOK LISTING EVERYTHING FROM THE LAWS AND ETHICS OF MAGIC AND SPELL-CASTING TO A NOTE OF THE SPELLS AND MAGIC THAT A WITCH HAS PERFORMED.

When new witches are welcomed into covens, it is said to be traditional for them to write their own Book of Shadows (although I personally doubt that witches kept such books in times past, because most of them couldn't read, and even if they could, being found with a book detailing magical procedures would have meant certain death during the burning time (see pages 18 to 22).

The original Book of Shadows is more likely to have been a mythical item or a term used to describe the attainment of wisdom and knowledge. In an interesting parallel, Native American legends tell of the *Book of Laws*, or *Book of Seals*, a mythical book that holds the laws of creation and is bound with crow's feathers (crows represent the law in Native American culture and are also considered shape-shifting, shadowy creatures).

You may, however, find it useful to keep a Book of Shadows for personal reference, but remember that you shouldn't show to anyone else, because this would break your power.

CHAPTER 2

THE WAYS OF WICCA

WE TEND TO THINK OF SCIENCE AS BEING A MODERN CONCEPT, BUT SCHOLARS, ALCHEMISTS, AND MAGICIANS HAVE PONDERED THE MYSTERIES OF MATTER AND EXISTENCE FOR CENTURIES. SUCH GREAT THINKERS OF THE PAST ARE OFTEN FORGOTTEN IN THIS MODERN AGE, YET THEIR GROUNDBREAKING WORK AND RESEARCH PAVED THE WAY FOR MANY OF THE SCIENTIFIC DISCOVERIES OF THE PAST CENTURY.

Although the scientific magic of the past has long been dismissed as superstition and mumbo jumbo, it is now making a comeback as a result of modern scientists' growing realization that many of its theories have a scientific basis. One occult theory that has been confirmed by science is that of ether, or "near matter", non-physical matter that has no form and that exists all around us, although we can neither see it, touch it, nor smell it. Having now discovered it, scientists today call it "dark matter".

Occult magic is the long-forgotten science of the past, and if we are to understand and use it we need to look at some of the fundamental concepts that form its basis.

THE ELEMENTS

AIR

FIRE

WATER

EARTH

In modern science, a hundred or so elements make up the periodic table, and although the elements are not so numerous in magic, they have great significance and importance. The concept of the four elements of air, fire, water, and earth exists in nearly every form of magic throughout the world, notable exceptions being the Chinese occult systems, such as Feng Shui, which use the five elements of wood, fire, earth, metal, and water.

The power of the elements is present all around us, yet most of us fail to notice it. How often have you heard someone described as having a fiery temper, for example? We use this kind of terminology every day, yet remain unaware of the truth at the core of what we are saying.

When you set out a circle for a spell-casting ceremony in Wiccan magic, tools placed at each point of the compass represent the elements, and when the metaphysical forces of these elements are combined they create a fifth element, which alchemists called ether, or "near matter". It is this fifth element that can be

ABOVE The element of fire represents drive and passion, but in extreme cases this can lead to bad-tempered behavior and conflict.

guided and molded by the intent of a spell, which then effects changes in the physical world (see page 28).

To assist you in your spell-casting, you need to understand what each of the four elements represents, such as a part of the body, a season, or even an emotional state. In addition, each of the four elements has a unique aspect and power, which our early ancestors linked with a particular god or deity.

Air

Air is the element of the east and is linked with springtime, new life, creativity, intelligence, and the logical, left-hand side of our brains. It is a masculine element and the domain of Paralda, lord of the entities of the air, which are referred to as sylphs. When casting a spell, air can be represented by an incense stick or oil-burner and, in Tarot decks, by the suit of swords (although swords are often associated with conflict, they are, in fact, representative of the mind and of the power of thought). In astrology, the element of air is linked with the zodiacal signs of Libra, Aquarius, and Gemini.

Fire

Fire is the element of the south and is linked with summer, energy, drive, passion, and the destruction of the old to make way for new growth. It is a masculine element and is ruled Djhinn (pronounced "gin"), lord of the entities

ABOVE Candles and fiery colors can help visualize the element of fire.

ABOVE LEFT The element of air is linked to springtime, creation and new beginnings.

of fire, or salamanders. When spell-casting, you can use a candle to represent fire and, in Tarot, the suit of wands (wands signify drive and new projects and, in terms of the human body, muscle and blood). Fire is also linked with the zodiacal signs of Sagittarius, Aries, and Leo.

ABOVE Various tools can be used to represent the element of air.

RIGHT When spell-casting, any container filled with water can be used to represent this element.

Water

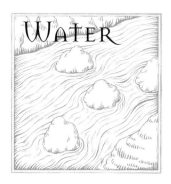

Water is the element of the west and is linked with autumn, empathy, love, emotions and the intuitive, right-hand side of the brain. It is a feminine element and is ruled by Nitsea, lord of the entities of water, or undines (sometimes called mermaids by sailors). When spell-casting, you can use almost any container filled with water to represent this element. In Tarot decks, water is represented by cups, the suit of emotions and love. The parts of the body ruled by the element of water are the digestive and reproductive systems. In astrology, water is linked with the zodiacal signs of Scorpio, Pisces, and Cancer.

Earth

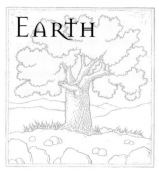

Earth is the element of the north and is linked with winter, solidity, stability, permanence, law, and the unchangeable. It is a feminine element and is ruled by Gob, lord of the entities of earth, or gnomes. When spell-casting, you can use a pentacle, or pentagram (see pages 66 to 67), or a container filled with earth or salt, to represent earth. In Tarot, earth is represented by the suit of coins (also called discs or stones). In the human body, earth is linked with the bones and skeletal structure. In astrology, earth's connection is with the zodiacal signs of Capricorn, Taurus, and Virgo.

ABOVE LEFT Autumn is the season linked to water, a time of reflection and conclusion after the dramatic time of mid-summer.

ABOVE Natural items (especially solid items like stones or wood!) and earthy color tones can be used to represent the element of earth.

ABOVE Anything linked to the sea, the coast, or even fishes can symbolize the element of water.

THE COLORS OF MAGIC

The world around us is full of color, and our ability to perceive different colors is a skill that sets us apart from much of the animal kingdom.

Colors have long been used in magic throughout the world. Followers of the Hindu faith, for example, believe in the chakras, the symbolically colored energy points of the human body. The Kabbala, the mystical tradition of the Jewish faith that shares many spiritual similarities with the Hindu faith, regards colors as spiritual forces or energies that can also be linked with the human body.

ABOVE The Hindu faith teaches the powers of the chakras, different colored points that are linked to human body.

ABOVE Color exists all around us, the rainbow is a natural symbol that has been used by various cultures to teach people about the different aspects of life and human existence.

BELOW The Jewish Kabbala or tree of life also uses color symbolism as an important teaching tool.

The use of colors as representative tools when spell-casting, meditating or balancing can be very important. If, for instance, you wish to use crystal or candle magic, when different-colored candles are used to symbolize a variety of emotions and ideas, the right choice of color is vital. Color can also play a significant role in balancing elements or setting the mood around your home (see pages 90 to 124). Indeed, color can affect our moods significantly, not just in magic, but in our day-to-day lives, too. The colors that they choose to wear, or to decorate their homes with, for instance, can say a lot about people.

LEFT Different-colored crystals can be used to create moods or emphasise certain influences in life.

The symbolic meanings associated with each color are detailed below.

WHITE

White is the color of the divine creative force and of the limitless power that it yields. White can also stand for childhood, new beginnings, purity, virginity, cleansing, innocence and peace. A white flag shown in wartime means that one side wants to stop fighting; a white dove is a universal symbol of peace. White is believed to form the basis of all of the other colors, except for black, which is thought to be an absence of light. When visionary magic is practiced, white robes are often worn, because white is thought to help to form a clear image in the mind's eye.

BLACK

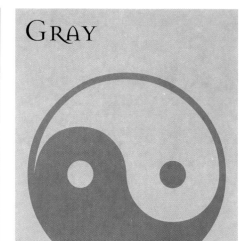

Naturally opposed to white, black is sometimes considered to be an absence of light, which is why many people associate it with all things sinister or evil (for example, black magic). Black is the color of the night and of unseen forces and can also represent fear of the unknown and death (although in almost all religions death is not the end, but a time of rest and regeneration before the birth of new life). In Egypt, the black mud of the river Nile once represented the cycle of life that was renewed each year, a symbolism shared by the dark moon and longest night in the Wiccan faith. Black can also mean binding, constraints and limitations. Its unique power is that it absorbs all of the other colors, and participants in many magical ceremonies often wear black to absorb the power of the spell.

GRAY

Sometimes described as a shade rather than a color, being a combination of black and white (yang and yin), gray can represent expectance, compromise and balance. Because it is also thought to be the color of invisibility and protection, visualizing a gray sphere around you can help you to avoid psychic attack or confrontation of any type, as well as aiding you in keeping secrets if you are being questioned.

YELLOW

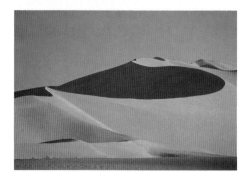

Yellow shares many symbolic properties with gold (see page 53) and orange (right), and can be the color of communication, of the mind, and of summer. It can also signify treachery and jealousy (in Western movies, a coward or traitor is often referred to as being "yellow", while in medieval paintings Judas is typically depicted wearing yellow clothes). Yellow can be linked with the sun, as well as with the planet Mercury. In magic, it is the color of intellect, learning, movement, and travel.

RED

Red is said to be the color of energy, vigor, passion, and desire. A fiery color, it can be linked with creation too. It is also thought to be an anger-inducing color, especially for Taureans, on whom it can act like a red rag to a bull. In magic, it can represent the ability to overcome difficult or trying situations. Beware of overexposing yourself to this color, however, for passion and desire can boil over if not kept in check.

ORANGE

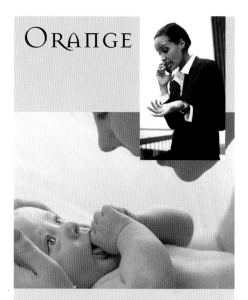

Sometimes linked with yellow and red (see left), orange is the color of intelligence and can also signify communication, being one of the colors associated with Mercury, the messenger of the Roman gods. In magic, orange is the color of joy, fertility, and personal happiness.

Green

Unsurprisingly, this color is said to represent nature, harmony, balance and fertile growth. It is the color of springtime, as well as of the Goddess (Mother Nature). It can be linked with the planet Venus, too, which, in magical terms, makes it the perfect color for finding new love or developing existing relationships.

Blue

Blue is sometimes thought to be the color of royalty (whose members are said to be blue-blooded) and represents wisdom, justice, loyalty and organization. It is linked with the planet Jupiter and the zodiacal sign Sagittarius, and is considered a healing, protective and feminine color. In magic, it can be used to expand boundaries and to help to find a sense of justice, especially if one is dealing with large organizations.

Purple

Along with blue, purple is considered a royal color and was traditionally worn by emperors, kings and priests. The color of the spirit and of the higher levels of existence, it represents tranquility and the trinity of the mind, body, and soul. It is also used to represent the fifth point of the pentagram (see pages 66 to 67). In magical practices, it can be used to help one to gain insight and strength of spirit.

BROWN

Brown is the color of the earth and represents affinity, intuitive communication and the absorption of knowledge (in Victorian times, studies were often painted brown for this very reason). It is linked with the zodiacal signs Libra, Scorpio, Capricorn, and Cancer. In magic, brown is a useful color that can keep one earthed and can help one to see the truth in a difficult situation when others are being misleading.

PINK

Like the color green, pink is linked with Venus and can also express love, but in a rather more kind and gentle way. It is a good color to turn to if one is suffering from insomnia because it can combat stress and helps to restore regular sleeping patterns. It can be used in magic to restore harmony if one has argued with a loved one.

GOLD

Gold, which is linked with almost all of the solar deities, such as Apollo and Ra, is the color of success and recognition. In magic, it can be used to promote confidence and the realization of ambition. It is also said to be one of the colors that symbolize money (another being silver) and is a good color to use when casting spells concerning money or success. Remember, however, that true achievement isn't always linked with money, although it can, of course, be very helpful!

SILVER

Linked with the Goddess and the moon, silver is the color of dreams and intuition, qualities that go beyond the physical and are more spiritual in nature. Because coins are often silver, it sometimes represents money, but when practicing magic it is best used to trigger sudden realizations and visions, especially in the form of dreams that can help one to see what is hidden in one's life.

MAGIC BY THE NUMBERS

The ability to count is something that sets us apart from animals. One of humankind's first

evolutionary steps, our early ancestors acquired this ability at about the same time that they

started to make tools and build communities. Being able to count helped them to understand the

cycles of the year and the movement of the planets, to discern patterns in the world around them,

and to unlock the mysteries of the universe.

In modern times, the science of pure mathematics has helped us to split the atom, to build

computers, and to ponder the possibilities of faster-than-light space travel. Yet the science of

mathematics is not a new concept: in 270 B.C. for example, Aristarchus of Samos, the Greek

astronomer, calculated the circumference of the Earth to within a few yards, using a pole,

two camels, and some rope.

The key difference between the mathematical science of today and the more ancient system of

Pythagorean numerology outlined below is that there are only single-digit numbers in Pythagorean

numerology, which means that there is no number higher than nine. In Pythagorean numerology,

each number (from one to nine inclusive) has symbolic significance, as detailed below.

ABOVE *The great scientific advances of the
last century were only made possible
because of the ground-breaking work of
the magicians of the past.*

ONE

The number one represents strength, inventiveness, creativity, and the beginning of a new cycle of events. It is a masculine number and is linked with the sun, the higher mind, and the divine force of God, as it is sometimes known.

TWO

Two is the number of polarity, cooperation and the coming together of two, often opposing, elements, such as male and female, and yin and yang, although this can sometimes bring about conflict. It is considered a feminine number and is linked with the new moon and the Goddess (in Tarot decks, it is the number of the High Priestess). Two symbolizes finding a balance in life, particularly in terms of relationships and human interaction. In magical practice, two candles of the appropriate colors represent two forces that can be brought together to work in cooperation, be it two people within a relationship or the mind and the body.

THREE

Three is the number of the trinity, the Triple Goddess, and the creation that occurs when two forces are united, for example, the child that is born after a man and woman have come together. Three has played an important symbolic role in nearly all world religions, and in a spiritual context it is the trinity of the mind, body, and soul. Thought to be a masculine number, three is linked with the planet Jupiter.

FOUR

Four is the number of Mother Earth and the four elements, and represents practicality, accomplishment, achievement, the law, balance, and stability. It can also signify the mundane, boring and routine, as well as the safety and security of the home.

FIVE

Five is a dramatic and exciting number, representing, as it does, change (either wanted or unwanted), expansion, messages, and communication. Also the number of the pentagram (see pages 66 to 67), five is linked with the planet Mercury, which is named for the messenger of the Roman gods.

SIX

Six is the number of harmony, emotions, kindness, love, friendship, and support. Six can also represent nostalgia or childhood and often symbolizes family or family-type relationships. A feminine number, six is linked with the planet Venus.

SEVEN

Seven is a very important number in Pythagorean numerology, which, like the three of the trinity, crops up in almost every world religion and belief system. (To give just a few examples, there are said to be seven heavens, seven archangels, seven deadly sins, seven virtues, seven colors of the rainbow, and seven planets.) Seven is the number of magic, endurance, choices, and challenges, and because it is the number of the full moon, it is considered a feminine number.

THE SEVEN COLORS OF THE RAINBOW

If you shine a light through a prism, the light is refracted into seven colors. A similar effect occurs in nature when a ray of sunlight pierces a cloud of a certain density to form a rainbow.

Early humans regarded this natural phenomenon as a mystical sign. Nordic peoples, for example, believed that the rainbow was the bridge to the world of the gods, because it was usually seen after a storm, which was thought to be caused by gods venting their anger. The appearance of the rainbow, therefore, was a sign that the gods were returning to their world. In the traditional belief of Ireland, the end of the rainbow is where leprechauns hide their gold, while in Judaeo-Christian belief, the rainbow is a sign of God's promise to Noah that the Earth will never again be flooded.

The Western world's use of the rainbow as a symbol of unity and freedom is probably derived from the Native American people's designation of it as a symbol of

equal human rights. Later adopted by the gay community, the rainbow is currently the symbol of the environmental organization Greenpeace.

Another level of the rainbow's symbolic significance lies in its seven colors, for the number seven is a key symbolic component in many religions, a number of whose writings refer to seven heavens and seven planets. In Christian belief, there are also seven archangels, seven virtues (faith, hope, charity, justice, prudence, temperance, and fortitude) and seven deadly sins (pride, avarice, lust, anger, sloth, gluttony, and envy).

Eight

Eight is the number of organization, structure, progress, and self-discipline, as well as of purpose and stability. It is considered a masculine number and is linked with the planet Saturn, the planet that regulates time and business.

Nine

Nine is the number of leadership, compassion, regeneration and healing. As the highest number in the Pythagorean system, it represents both the end of a cycle and old age. Nine is said to be a "perfect" number because it is made up of three trinities ($3 \times 3 = 9$). It is also regarded as the number of fate because when any number is added to it, the total can be broken down to reveal that number again, for instance, $4 + 9 = 13$, $1 + 3 = 4$. A masculine number, nine is linked with the planet Mars.

NUMEROLOGY AND MAGIC

To use numerology to determine which number you are governed by (sometimes called your "lucky" number), all that you have to do is to add up the numbers that make up your date of birth.

For example, if you were born on 8.7.1978, add those numbers together (8 + 7 + 1 + 9 + 7 + 8 = 40), then add the numbers that make up the total (40) together (you may have to do this more than once) to give a single digit (4 + 0 = 4). Your number is therefore 4.

Numerology can also be a useful tool for divination. If you have a question that you'd like answered, for instance, take a set of dice, focus on the question in your mind, roll the dice, add up the numbers shown, and then reduce them to a single figure by adding them together, for example, 5 + 6 = 11, 1 + 1 = 2. This number indicates the answer to your question.

You can also use numerology to discover what a certain day, say 12.8.2003, has in store for you. To do this, simply add the numbers that make up the date together (1 + 2 + 8 + 2 + 0 + 0 + 3 = 16), then reduce the total to a single digit (1 + 6 = 7). The number that rules 12.8.2003 is therefore seven, and looking up its symbolic associations (see page 57) will give you an indication of what the day will be like.

For a more detailed interpretation, you could identify the day's—and perhaps also a particular hour's—ruling planet (see pages 82 to 87), too.

Because the various influences that govern a day can affect the outcome of a spell, it's best to pick the most auspicious day (and maybe also the hour) that you can for spell-casting. Do this by cross-referencing the information yielded by identifying a day's ruling planet (and perhaps hour) and number.

Tools, talismans, and symbols

When spell-casting, you can use various tools to help you to visualize the intent of a spell, such as candles, crystals (see the section on colors, pages 49 to 53), cards, rune stones, talismans, and symbols.

Because magic is a very personal skill, you can use whatever tool you feel works for you best.

That having been said, certain tools generally work well because of their cultural relevance to you, namely those symbols and charms that your cultural ancestors used for centuries and that have become engrained in your tribal memory.

Due to the complex nature of society, you can probably trace your roots back to many different cultures and civilizations, which means that finding the tool that works best for you may require a little trial and error. On reading through this book, you may come across certain tools that you feel familiar with, even if you have never consciously seen them before. This may be an indication of a tribal memory being stirred. So, if you learn to trust and follow your instincts, more often than not you'll find them to be right.

BELOW Rune stones from the Nordic culture have always been associated with magic and also form the basis of most of the European alphabetic languages.

ABOVE Whatever tools you use to help you with your magic, try to find items that have a certain sort relevance to you—this could be cultural or personal.

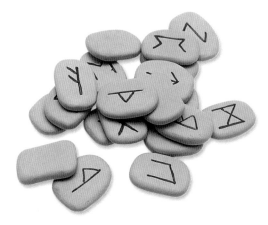

MAGICAL TOOLS

The use of cards and rune stones for predicting the future is well known, but they can also be used to represent whatever it is that you want from a spell. If you have ever had, or have done, a reading, you will understand that the cards or rune stones used are laid out in a certain order so that they relay the story of what is currently going on, or what will happen. When you use these types of tools for spell-casting, however, you should lay them out to create a story that illustrates what you want your spell to achieve.

Although Tarot is the best-known divinatory card system, it is only one of many, and, in fact, you can use almost any type of deck to help you with visualization (whatever type of card system you buy, it will normally be accompanied by a booklet that explains the meaning of each card and the various spreads that you can lay out). When spell-casting, use such cards to indicate what you want to happen, or the intent of the spell, rather than what is currently happening or will happen in the future.

Another type of visualization tool is a fith-fath, or an effigy of the person for whom you are casting a spell. You may be familiar with the voodoo curse that involves sticking pins into a doll to make the victim feel pain or fall ill, but this goes against the ethics of spell-casting (see page 31), and fith-faths should only be used for beneficial purposes, such as healing and encouraging love and prosperity.

ABOVE RIGHT here are many other types of divination cards, some use animal or Shamanic symbolism and you may find this type of imagery easier to use.

ABOVE Tarot cards are a well-known divination tool, but they can also be used for visualization.

Fith-faths are often carved from wax, but if this sounds too difficult, you could always adapt a plastic doll or figure. All that you have to do is to personalize it so that it represents the person in question, which shouldn't take long if you focus on a characteristic, perhaps a hairstyle or an article of clothing, that you associate with that person.

There are various ways of using fith-faths, nearly all of which should be undertaken within the circle (see pages 34 to 35). Like all tools, fith-faths must be charged with energy before they are used, which you should do by taking them and then bowing to the four points of the compass in turn. When doing this with a fith-fath, you must state who it represents and what you want your spell to achieve. For example, when making your bow, say, "O power of the [state the name of the direction] and the element of [state the name of the element], let this be [state the name of the person represented by the fith-fath] so that I can [state whatever it is that you want your spell to achieve]."

What you do next depends on your spell's intent. You could tie a ribbon around the fith-fath (the color of the ribbon should be appropriate to the type of spell, see pages 49 to 53), for instance, or you could tie two fith-faths together with a pink or green ribbon if you're casting a love spell.

LEFT Dolls can be used as visualization tools, but remember to try and personalize them.

RIGHT For love spells you could use two dolls to represent the two people you want to bring together.

MAGICAL TALISMANS

Talismans are useful magical tools that can be used to protect, find love or encourage prosperity. A talisman is basically a personalized form of spell that can be worn by a person or animal and can also be placed around the home (see page 106).

To create a talisman, you'll need a piece of paper or parchment, but must first work out what it is that you want it to achieve, as you would with any spell. Do this by considering the influence of each of the planets (see pages 82 to 87) and then deciding which best suits your purposes. Now identify the planetary square that applies to that particular planet (see pages 63 to 64) and then work out the numerical value of each of the letters that make up the name of the person for whom you are making the talisman (see page 63). As a general rule, use the name this person likes to be known by—first, last or nickname.

RIGHT Planetary squares are extremely old magical symbols and are based on the mathematical calculations of the orbit of a particular planet.

37	78	29	70	21	62	20	54	5
6	38	79	30	71	22	63	14	46
47	7	39	80	31	72	23	55	15
16	48	8	40	81	32	64	24	56
57	17	49	9	41	73	33	65	25
26	58	18	50	1	42	74	34	66
67	27	59	10	51	2	43	75	35
36	68	19	60	11	52	3	44	76
77	28	69	20	61	12	53	4	45

THE SQUARE OF SATURN

4	9	2
3	5	7
8	1	6

THE SQUARE OF JUPITER

4	14	15	1
9	7	6	12
5	11	10	8
16	2	3	13

THE SQUARE OF MARS

11	24	7	20	3
4	12	25	8	16
17	5	13	21	9
10	18	1	14	22
23	6	19	2	15

THE SQUARE OF THE SUN

6	32	3	34	35	1
7	11	27	28	8	30
19	14	16	15	23	24
18	20	22	21	17	13
25	29	10	9	26	12
36	5	33	4	2	31

THE SQUARE OF VENUS

22	47	16	41	10	35	4
5	23	48	17	42	11	29
30	6	24	49	18	36	12
13	31	7	25	43	19	37
38	14	32	1	26	44	20
21	39	8	33	2	27	45
46	15	40	9	34	3	28

THE SQUARE OF MERCURY

8	58	59	5	4	62	63	1
49	15	14	52	53	11	10	56
41	23	22	44	45	19	18	48
32	34	35	29	28	38	39	25
40	26	27	37	36	30	31	33
17	47	46	20	21	43	42	24
9	55	54	12	13	51	50	16
64	2	3	61	60	6	7	57

THE SQUARE OF THE MOON

37	78	29	70	21	62	13	54	5
6	38	79	30	71	22	63	14	46
47	7	39	80	31	72	23	55	15
16	48	8	40	81	32	64	24	56
57	17	49	9	41	73	33	65	25
26	58	18	50	1	42	74	34	66
67	27	59	10	51	2	43	75	35
36	68	19	60	11	52	3	44	76
77	28	69	20	61	12	53	4	45

THE VALUE OF LETTERS

1	2	3	4	5
A	B	C	D	E
J	K	L	M	N
S	T	U	V	W

6	7	8	9
F	G	H	I
O	P	Q	R
X	Y	Z	

The best way to charge up your talisman with power is to use the spell described in Chapter 1 (see page 34 to 37). Once you've encircled yourself in a ring of protection and have bowed to the four powers, take a pen and bow to them again. Now take your piece of paper or parchment and do the same, repeating the procedure with a candle, whose color should normally be that associated with the planet that you are working with (see pages 82 to 87), although it may be differ according to the intent of the spell.

The next step is to take the candle and to place it in front of you, saying, "I light this candle as the power of [state the name of the planet that you are working with]." Then lay the paper or parchment over the planetary square and, using the pen, trace out the numbers of the letters that make up the name of the person for whom the talisman is intended (if you prefer, you could mark them out lightly with a pencil first), saying, "I charge this talisman with power in the name of [state the name of the planet] for [state the name of the person] to [state the talisman's intent]."

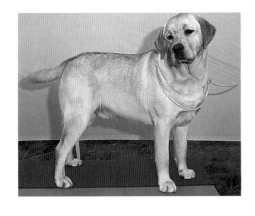

ABOVE *Animal symbolism exists in every culture, dogs, for instance, can be used to represent loyalty or protection depending on which culture you are looking at.*

Now add any symbol that represents what you want the talisman to achieve, such as an acorn for new beginnings (acorns symbolize the emergence of new life) or a dog for protection and loyalty.

Finally fold the paper, the number of times you fold it can also be important (see Magic by the numbers, pages 54 to 59), each square is linked to a planet and each has a number (i.e. 1=Sun, 2=Moon, 3=Jupiter, and so on), and you could try folding to the number of the planet.

Then seal the talisman with some wax from the candle, saying "I seal this spell" and close the spell by blowing out the candle, at the same time saying "Amen" (which means "So be it") or something similar.

The talisman can then either be bound or placed in a pouch to keep it safe, then it can either be worn or placed somewhere around the home, depending on what you want it for.

ABOVE *The sealing of the talisman is very important as, symbolically, it closes this type of spell.*

MAGICAL SYMBOLS

Symbols communicate various messages to us every day. Whether they take the form of national flags

or road signs, for example, symbols send non-verbal messages to our brains. In magical practices,

symbols perform a similar function, although the messages that they relay are far more powerful.

The symbol that most often springs to mind in association with witchcraft, and one of the most controversial, is the sign of the pentagram. The Christian Church often identifies the pentagram with devil-worship, but being that the devil is purely a Christian concept, it follows that this facet of the pentagram's symbolism is a Christian invention. Indeed, it is a little-known fact that the pentagram was used in the worship of Christ by some factions of the early Christian Church, and similarly is used as an aid to worship within the Jewish and Muslim faiths.

ABOVE Symbols are used every day to communicate messages to us, these can be road signs, billboards or flags.

The pentagram is, in fact, an ancient symbol that is much older than any of these religions. And, although its true origins have been lost in the mists of time, its significance and importance cannot be questioned or over-looked. In witchcraft, the five points of the pentagram represent the four points of the compass and the four elements, combined with the human spirit (the fifth point). The combination of the higher human mind with the elements forms the basis of many magical ceremonies because it creates ether (see page 46). The pentagram can be used for invoking powers (see pages 39 to 40), for protection (see pages 34 to 35) or can be worn to convey the message that the wearer is a witch.

Another well-known symbol, but one endorsed by the Christian Church, is the sign of the cross, which, in Christianity, represents the cross on which Christ was crucified. In fact, the cross is a far more ancient symbol than Christianity. As Christianity spread across Europe, the Christian Church was compelled to borrow the symbols of the older faiths that it was unable to eradicate, including the cross,

which, in Celtic culture, was often enclosed within a circle, representing the creation of the circle of life through the unification of the four elements.

The circle is one of the most overlooked symbols of all, and although its importance has already been touched upon, it would be impossible to do it justice within a few pages. The circle, which has no beginning or end, represents the reality of existence and time. Mathematically perfect, and yet imperfect, it is impossible to work out any of its dimensions to the last digit because it just goes on and on. It is said that the invention of the wheel was the most important evolutionary step that our species ever made. This may well be true, but its importance doesn't simply lie in its ability to transport people and goods, for the wheel, or circle, was one of the first symbols that humankind discovered could be used for teaching.

ABOVE The Christian symbol of the cross is, in fact, a much older than the Christian faith.

RIGHT The Celtic cross represents the coming together of the four elements, creating the circle of life. This powerful symbol was taken and adapted by the Catholic church as it moved northward into Celtic Europe.

CHAPTER 3

The Times for Magic

It is said that our universe is governed by time, and that no matter where we live in the world, our lives are also governed by time. The Babylonians of the ancient world were masters of magic and developed the way in which we measure time in the twenty-first century. Because they counted in sixes, today we use a system that has sixty seconds in a minute, sixty minutes in an hour and twenty-four hours (4 x 6 = 24) in a day.

The way in which a culture marks the passage of time often forms the basis of its religious beliefs and system of magic. This is evident in the obvious link between astrology and the Tarot. In order to understand magic better, we therefore need to look at time and the different methods that we use to mark its passing

THE WICCAN CALENDAR

The Wiccan year is symbolized by the "witches' wheel", whose eight spokes mark the eight important festivals of the witches' year, four of which are solar and four lunar. In times past, these were the most important dates in the farming year, and, because the survival of early communities was more closely linked with the land than it is today, an understanding of the seasons and what they represented was considered vital. Although relatively few of us are today dependent on farming (or the land) by comparison, learning to understand the significance of each of the festivals can help us better understand the links that we still share with the forces of Mother Nature.

BELOW One of the main benefits the Wiccan faith has had on modern day life is farming, the religious festivals of the Wiccan calendar were used to mark out the farming year and teach our forefathers about the cycles of the seasons.

The wheel represents more than just the passing of the seasons. It symbolizes the times of the day, from morning to night, the phases of our lives, from birth to death, and also shows that everything in our lives has a beginning and an end. Be it in terms of our personal relationships or the challenges and tasks that we find ourselves facing, everything begins, moves through a series of different phases, and then ends to make way for the new. When you look at the wheel and apply it to your life, you will start to see where you are now and where you are going. As time moves on, so do we, and understanding the cycle of the wheel can help us to gain insight into our lives and thus attain greater wisdom. But remember that the wheel is always turning, and that just as one thing ends, something new begins.

As you study the ancient religious significance of the festivals outlined below, you will start to understand how the witches' wheel helped to educate the population, not only about farming practices and working with the seasons, but also about the cycle of existence. The abandonment and misuse of these festivals have caused us to lose touch with the world in which we live, contributing to the destruction that humankind is wreaking on our ecosystem. We need to realize that we are as much a part of our planet as a blade of grass or grain of sand. Everything has its place in the great scheme of things, but it appears that we have lost ours, and if our species wishes to survive, we must repair the link that we once shared with our planet.

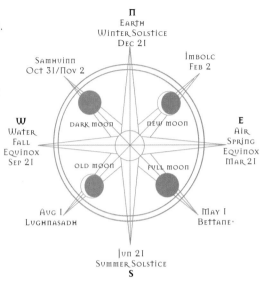

ABOVE *The witches' wheel helped our ancestors to understand the cycles of life and death.*

Please note, dates may change, as the solstices equinoxes can vary from year to year.

As the Earth moves on its axis orbiting the sun, the amount of sunlight that we receive changes throughout the year. The four solar festivals mark these changes as the turning points of the seasons, and are celebrated as important times of the natural year in most cultures. The solar festivals also represent the cycles of the sun, the most important and powerful natural force in our lives. If you dispute this observation, just ask yourself what would happen if the sun failed to dawn in the morning. In fact, not that many millions of years ago, the dinosaurs encountered just that problem, when the debris from an asteroid strike was thrown up into the atmosphere, blotting out the light of the sun. Within three months any forms of life that hadn't died due to the huge drop in temperature began to starve as the food chain broke down. In that devastation, nearly 90 percent of life on Earth was wiped out (but then the human race evolved from those animal forms that did survive, so in a way it wasn't such a bad thing, for us, at least).

You may not grow your own food, but everything that you eat and drink, and much of what you wear, is the result of farming of some kind, an industry that remains dependent on the sun and the changing of the seasons. Our ancestors knew this, and honored the solar festivals and the changing seasons of the year as part of the cycle of life and death.

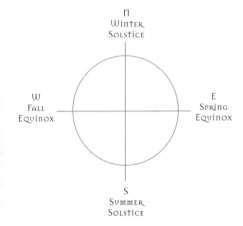

ABOVE *By learning to understand the seasons our ancestors turned from being hunter-gatherers to being farmers.*

The Winter Solstice

The solar festivals start on December 21 with the winter solstice, the time when the nights are at their longest and the sun is at its weakest. Because the winter solstice marks the end of the darkest quarter of the year, it is a time of new beginnings, conception, incarnation, and hope. As the old saying goes, "It is always darkest before the dawn", and from now on the days will start to lengthen and life will begin to burgeon again within the earth.

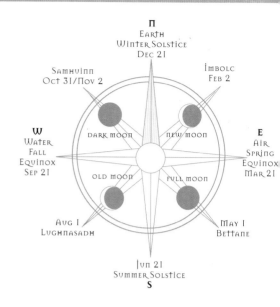

This scenario of hope is paralleled in the Christian calendar by Christmas (although Christmas is celebrated on December 25, the Christian Church "borrowed" an older festival). On Christmas Day, the sense of hope and joy that is instilled by the lengthening of the days is represented by the birth of Christ, the son of God and savior of humankind.

On the witches' wheel, the winter solstice is in the north.

ABOVE The winter solstice is a time of endings and beginnings. The old gives way to the new and, linked to the summer solstice, the winter solstice marks the time of conception of the next generation.

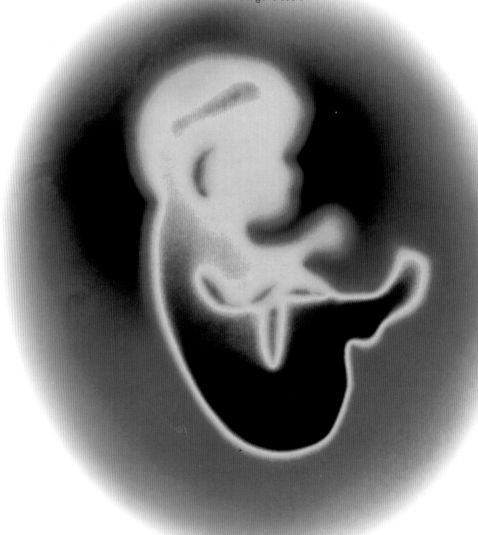

ABOVE The sense of hope symbolized in the Christian festival of Christmas was originally the Wiccan winter solstice.

On the witches' wheel diagram:

- **Ⅱ** EARTH WINTER SOLSTICE DEC 21
- SAMHUINN OCT 31/NOV 2
- IMBOLC FEB 2
- **W** WATER FALL EQUINOX SEP 21
- DARK MOON
- NEW MOON
- **E** AIR SPRING EQUINOX MAR 21
- OLD MOON
- FULL MOON
- AUG 1 LUGHNASADH
- MAY 1 BELTANE
- JUN 21 SUMMER SOLSTICE **S**

THE SPRING EQUINOX

The spring equinox is celebrated on March 21, when the day and night are equal in length (each lasting twelve hours). The days will soon outlast the nights, however, as the season of summer approaches. This time can be compared to a child who will soon travel the journey of wisdom on the way toward adulthood. At this time of year, crops were once sown and and celebrations held for the coming of summer.

ABOVE *On the witches' wheel, the spring equinox is in the east.*

The Christian festival of Easter, which is traditionally held on the first Sunday after the first new moon following the spring equinox, is another example of a Christian festival that is based on a much older, pagan tradition. The Easter bunny was once the hare of the Saxon goddess Eostre, who gave her name to this Christian festival. Sometimes called the corn spirit, the hare represented new life and spring growth. The painted eggs that are associated with Easter are ancient symbols of fertility, derived from the once widespread belief in Britain that hares lay eggs (this belief arose because hares sleep in nest-like structures called "forms" that have more than a passing resemblance to lapwing nests).

On the witches' wheel, the spring equinox is in the east.

ABOVE *The Easter festival, celebrated on the first Sunday after the new moon that follows the spring equinox, is actually the old Saxon festival of the Goddess Eostre.*

RIGHT *The spring equinox symbolizes the fertiliy, birth and growth of new life. This can be seen in the imagery of the Easter festival i.e. new-born lambs, eggs, and rabbits (originally hares!).*

The summer solstice

The summer solstice is celebrated on June 21, the longest day of the year, when the sun is at its most powerful. This is summer time, symbolically the time of the adult, when men and women would traditionally come together to conceive the next generation, and crop growth would by now have been well established in preparation for the fall harvest.

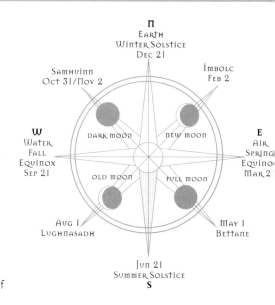

Although the sun's power is at its peak, the summer solstice also marks the time when its force starts to grow weaker, which is why people would begin to make preparations for the coming of winter to ensure the survival of the babies and young animals who were born at the time of Imbolc (see page 77).

BELOW The mid-summer solstice marks the time of the summer harvests as the days start to grow shorter.

RIGHT Summer is a time of energy and excitement as the power of the sun reaches its peak.

BELOW The summer solstice is also the time when adult and couples would come together to create the next generation of life.

Π
Earth
Winter Solstice
Dec 21

Samhuinn
Oct 31/Nov 2

Imbolc
Feb 2

DARK MOON

NEW MOON

W
Water
Fall
Equinox
Sep 21

E
Air
Spring
Equinox
Mar 21

OLD MOON

FULL MOON

Aug 1
Lughnasadh

May 1
Beltane

Jun 21
Summer Solstice
S

ABOVE On the witches' wheel, the spring equinox is in the west

The fall equinox

The fall equinox is celebrated on September 21, when the days and nights are equal in length, as on the spring equinox. The wheel of the year is turning toward its darkest quarter, however, and the nights will soon begin to grow longer and the days shorter and darker.

The life that first appeared in the spring now starts to return to the earth as the year begins to die, the last of the harvests having already been gathered in and stored for the coming winter. This is the time of maturity and of reflection on the year that has passed.

At this point in the year, the tribal leader would once have been judged on the year's events and, following a bad year, the chief would sometimes have had to make the ultimate sacrifice and submit to a ceremonial killing. Evidence for this has been discovered in the form of bodies found in peat bogs across Europe. Because the hands of these sacrificial victims show no signs of damage from hard labor, it is fair to assume that they were not simple peasants, but people who served a high function within their communities, in some cases perhaps even being the tribal leaders. This rather harsh form of democracy formed the basis of the structure of governance and introduced the concept of the sacrificial king, giving us some idea of the role and responsibility of the monarch in European society at a time when the king and the land were thought to be as one. (See also pages 10 to 11).

ABOVE LEFT The fall equinox marks the time of maturity in our lives when wisdom of the older generation is passed onto the younger generation.

LEFT The life that first appeared in the spring now starts to return to the earth as the days get shorter and colder.

RIGHT The last of the harvest would be gathered in and preparations would be made for the coming winter.

The Lunar Festivals

The lunar festivals do not mark the seasons so much as the phases of life, both of humans, and of animals. In times past, these festivals helped our ancestors to ascertain when to turn out their livestock to summer or winter pasture, and when their animals should be born or killed.

Although not as powerful as the sun, the moon still performs a number of vital functions: without its gravitational pull the Earth wouldn't rotate on its axis and there would be no seasons, the days and nights would be of equal length (as they are on the equinoxes), and life may not have evolved in the way that it has.

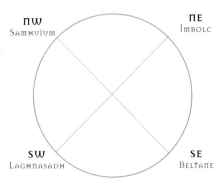

ABOVE The lunar festivals mark the times of life from birth during the time of Imbolc to death during the time of Samhuinn.

ABOVE The moon has a very dramatic affect on our lives; it's gravitational pull affects the tides which in turn affects the changing weather patterns of the seasons.

BELOW The worshipping of the moon (the Goddess) was thought to encourage better weather during the farming year. If the year was marked by bad weather (i.e. snow) then the tribal chief was often sacrificed to appease the Goddess.

The power of the moon also directs the tides of the great oceans, in turn affecting the winds and rains that arrive with the passing of the seasons, whose importance to the farming year our ancestors understood. If the rains came late in spring, for example, crop growth would be affected for the rest of the year, while if the summer was very wet, or the snows too heavy in winter, the crops could fail, causing the animals and people who depended on them for survival to starve. These seasonal weather changes remain important today, affecting as they do the production of food across the world.

These lunar festivals were once used as teaching tools, not only to provide instruction about farming, but also about life itself, from birth to death through all of the intervening phases.

Diagram

Π
Earth
Winter Solstice
Dec 21

Samhuinn
Oct 31/Nov 2

Imbolc
Feb 2

W
Water
Fall
Equinox
Sep 21

DARK MOON · NEW MOON

OLD MOON · FULL MOON

E
Air
Spring
Equinox
Mar 21

Aug 1
Lughnasadh

May 1
Beltane

Jun 21
Summer Solstice
S

Imbolc

The cycle of lunar festivals starts with Imbolc, which is celebrated on February 2. This festival marks the time when winter begins to lessen its grip and the first signs of the new life that was conceived on the summer solstice (see page 74) start to emerge, with the birth of young animals and sprouting of plants. This is the time of the child and of dependence, for a child is dependent on its parents.

ABOVE On the witches' wheel, Imbolc is in the north-east.

BELOW RIGHT Plant life would also start to emerge from the earth after the long cold winter.

BOTTOM RIGHT This is also the time of the child, though still totally dependent on their parents, these children would grow and ensure the generations to come.

BELOW Imbolc is the time of birth—the livestock of the new generation would be born, marking the start of the farming year.

At Imbolc, when a sense of hope for the future would prevail, celebrations would be held to celebrate these new beginnings in the name of the goddess Bridget.

On the witches' wheel, Imbolc is in the north-east.

BELTANE

Beltane is celebrated on May 1 (May Day, which is today a public holiday throughout much of the Western world). This is the first day of summer, when livestock would traditionally be walked between two huge bonfires as a form of cleansing ritual after the long winter, before being turned out to summer pasture. Food would be more plentiful at this time of year, and life would be filled with joy, due to the arrival of summer.

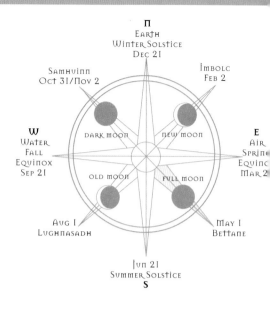

Beltane is also considered the time of lovers because the fire of passion starts to grow as youth moves toward adulthood. It is a time of independence, too, because the child, having grown into an adult, is no longer reliant on its parents and family for survival.

Due to its links with Samhuinn (see page 80), it was thought that the gates of the spirit world opened at Beltane, enabling communion to take place with long-dead ancestors.

On the witches' wheel, Beltane is in the south-east.

ABOVE On the witches' wheel, the winter solstice is in the south-east.

RIGHT Beltane falls on May 1 and symbolizes the time of the lovers as the young would start to gather in a celebration of fertility.

BOTTOM RIGHT The celebrations also marked a time of independence as the children moved toward adulthood and no longer needed their parents.

The witches' wheel diagram:

Π
Earth
Winter Solstice
Dec 21

Samhuinn
Oct 31/Nov 2

Imbolc
Feb 2

W
Water
Fall
Equinox
Sep 21

Dark moon — New moon

E
Air
Spring
Equinox
Mar 21

Old moon — Full moon

Aug 1
Lughnasadh

May 1
Beltane

Jun 21
Summer Solstice
S

Lughasadh

Lughasadh, which is celebrated on August 1, is the time of the family, marriage, and business. The first of the harvests would be gathered in now, with the year being judged on their success. (The success or failure of the harvest was often seen as a reflection of the leadership of the community, and in a bad year the replacement of the old tribal chief by a successor would be considered.)

ABOVE On the witches' wheel, the spring equinox is in the south-west.

BELOW Lughasadh is the time of the marriage, as couples sealed love with a commitment of love.

Lughasadh is linked with Imbolc in the north-east as a time of dependence, but this time it is the dependence of parents, having grown older and weaker, on their children.

On the witches' wheel, Lughasadh is in the south-west.

TOP This was also the time of the parent, the commitment of marriage ultimately leading to the birth of the next generation of children.

ABOVE The summer now turns to fall, and the crops of summer would now start to be gathered in to prepare for the long winter months.

Samhuinn

More commonly known as Halloween, the festival of Samhuinn is still celebrated today, although much of its true significance has been lost and it is now little more than an excuse for children to cause mayhem.

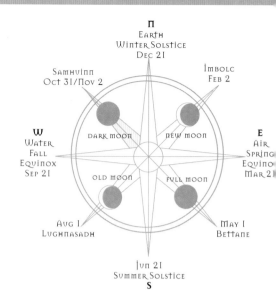

Samhuinn is traditionally a three-day festival that starts on October 31 and ends on November 2.

As well as marking the witches' new year, Samhuinn signifies the end of the old farming year and the beginning of the new, when the first of the winter crops would be sown for germination in the spring of the coming year.

Over these three days normal business would be suspended and chaos would reign throughout the community, with men dressed as women, and women as men, knocking on doors

ABOVE *On the witches' wheel, Samhuinn is in the north-west. Because this area of the witches' wheel is open to these mercurial forces, when translated to the home, it is an area that needs protecting (see page 117).*

BELOW *This festival is now more commonly know as Halloween and marks the darkest quarter of the year.*

asking for food (this is the origin of the practise of trick-or-treating). Because Samhuinn falls in the middle of the darkest quarter of the year, such frivolity played an important part in lifting the mood of the people, helping to protect them from the negative forces that wander the Earth at this time of year.

Although it is linked with Beltane in the south-east as a time of independence, in this instance it is the total independence that comes with death, which is why Samhuinn is sometimes considered an evil time. Because it signifies the opening of the gateway to the spirit or other

ABOVE The tradition of trick-or-treating was born out of the chaos that reigned during this time.

ABOVE This three-day festival marked the opening of the gateways to the next life and the time of independence from life.

world, when spirits can wander freely in this world, it gives an opportunity for communion with long-dead ancestors. Contact with the spirits can be a good or bad thing, however, depending on the nature of the spirits. On the witches' wheel, Samhuinn is in the north-west.

Because this area of the witches' wheel is open to these mercurial forces, when translated to the home, it is an area that needs protecting (see page 117).

Days, hours, and the planets

Astrology is one of the few remnants of ancient magic that is still evident in society today, with horoscopes being printed in many daily newspapers and even featuring on some radio and television programs. Although many people dismiss astrology as simply a bit of fun, the planets can, in fact, have a very powerful influence on our daily lives.

Timing is everything, or so it is said, and magic is no different in this respect. Because picking the right day or hour can have a markedly positive effect on your magic, try to identify the correct moment to cast your spell. If you are new to witchcraft and are unsure when best to cast a spell, however, start at the beginning, with the sun, and you shouldn't go too far wrong.

The planetary days

Before the advent of the telescope, there were thought to be only seven planets, which were accordingly believed to rule and influence the seven days of the week. Indeed, many days are still known by their planetary names, for example, Sunday (the sun's day), Monday (the moon's day) and Saturday (Saturn's day).

Each of the seven planets has a unique set of characteristics that influence the day with which the planet is associated, as follows.

SUNDAY:
THE DAY OF THE SUN

Traditionally the first day of the week, Sunday was once sacred to Mithras, the god of the Mithraic solar cult of ancient Rome that later went on to form part of the basis of the Roman Catholic Church, when it became the last day of the week and the day of rest. This sacred day is linked with the divine creative force and, because everything was ultimately given life by the sun, symbolizes the beginning and origin of all things.

Because it is associated with hope and optimism for the future, it is a good day to plan or start projects. Spells linked with any new venture should similarly be cast on this day.

MONDAY:
THE DAY OF THE MOON

Because the moon is the second-most important astrological body, it makes sense that it should rule the second day of the week. While the sun is masculine and active, the moon is feminine and reflective, making Monday an emotional and feminine day, and a good one on which to reflect on times or memories that have touched your emotions.

Monday is the best day for casting spells that are linked with emotional issues, but take care, because your emotions may spill over, causing moodiness or depression, and you may not find yourself in the right frame of mind for spell-casting!

TUESDAY:
THE DAY OF MARS

Named after Tyr, the Nordic god of war, the third day of the week is ruled by the fiery and masculine planet Mars (in Roman mythology, also the god of war). This is a day of activity, when the force of your will can achieve almost anything, be it good or bad (the power and drive that Tuesday brings can either result in success or cause conflict).

If you need to cast a spell to help you to deal with a difficult situation, this is the day to do it, but take care because Tuesday's power can go too far, causing problems.

WEDNESDAY:
THE DAY OF MERCURY

Deriving its name from the Anglo-Saxon god Wodan, Odin, the chief of the Nordic gods, communication, and travel are the influences of the day of Mercury. These influences can be very useful if the force of Mars' day, Tuesday, has led to arguments because they can help you to talk things over and, if that doesn't work, to extricate yourself from any trouble.

An excellent day for casting spells relating to travel or holidays, it is also a good one on which to cast spells to help you get in touch with old friends or people with whom you may need to talk.

THURSDAY:
THE DAY OF JUPITER

Thursday is another day that takes its name from one of the Nordic gods, in this case Thor, the god of thunder and lightning, while as far as the ancient Romans were concerned, this was the day of Jupiter, the king of their gods. Thursday can bring both good and bad luck, and is an auspicious day on which to expand on your ideas and learn more about the world.

Thursday is a day for casting spells concerned with organization, and if you need to deal with large institutions, this is the day to do so.

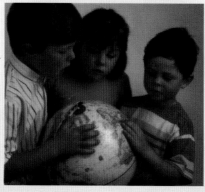

FRIDAY:
THE DAY OF VENUS

The Romans called this day Veneris, the day of Venus. When their empire spread northward, the Norse races that they conquered linked this day with the goddess Frigg, or Freyja (in whose honor fish was originally eaten on Fridays), whose characteristics closely resembled those of Venus. This is the day of love, and of the consequences of love, be they good or bad.

Friday is accordingly a good day on which to express your feelings or to meet a loved one, and is also the best day for casting love spells.

SATURDAY: THE DAY OF SATURN

The last day of the week is governed by Saturn, the planet of time (and some say that Saturn is one of the names of the force that created the universe because it is governed by time). Being the last day of the week, Saturday is traditionally the day of endings, making it the best day for finishing things, especially difficult things that you have been avoiding.

Saturday is not a day for starting projects, and to do so is thought to bring bad luck, which means that spells shouldn't usually be cast on this day. If you have been going through a rough time, however, Saturday could be a good day to cast a spell to put an end to it.

THE PLANETARY HOURS

Just as the days of the week are governed by the planets, so are the hours of the day, although the planets' order of influence may differ slightly. The influence of a particular planet over a certain hour can dramatically affect the outcome of a spell, as indicated below.

To find the planetary hour of a certain day of the week, you need to know that the first hour after sunrise is ruled by the same planet that rules the day, for example, the first hour after sunrise on a Sunday is the hour of the sun because Sunday is the day of the sun. This convention stems from the ancient Greeks, who believed that the day began at dawn (although it was considered to start at sunset in some northern cultures).

If you want to find the planetary ruler of an hour after sunset, you need to start by identifying the planet that rules that day and then count through the cycle of hours in the order given below until you reach the sixth hour. For a Sunday, for example, you would start with the hour of the sun and then count through the hours until you come to the sixth hour, which is the hour of Jupiter, making the first hour after sunset on a Sunday the hour of Jupiter.

It is important to appreciate the importance of the planetary hours when you are spell-casting. If you want to cast a love spell, for instance, it is recommended that you cast it during the hour of Venus (Venus being the planet of love); alternatively, if you haven't spoken to someone for a long time, but would welcome it if he or she got in touch with you, then the hour of Mercury (Mercury being the planet of communication) would be the best time to cast a spell with that intent.

The hour of the sun

All things ultimately come from the sun: everything in our solar system, all of our light and energy, even the very matter that we are made up of. The sun therefore represents the divine father of all creation.

The hour of the sun is a good time to cast spells relating to new projects, love or prosperity.

The hour of Venus

Because Venus was the Roman goddess of love, her hour is accordingly associated with love, romance, partnerships and women.

This a good hour during which to cast not only love spells, but also any spell relating to emotions or women.

The hour of Mercury

Mercury was the messenger of the Roman gods, and his hour denotes communication and travel.

This is the best hour to cast spells relating to a holiday, business trip or anything linked with communication, be it associated with business or friendship.

The hour of the moon

The moon is the symbol of the Goddess and represents the instinctive, the unconscious, and the mother of creation.

This is a good hour to cast both love spells (especially on a new or full moon) and fertility spells, because the phases of the moon, which range from new to full, can symbolize the stages of a woman's pregnancy.

The hour of Saturn

The hour of Saturn is governed by the planet of time.

Although it is a good hour to cast spells that bring organization and status, it may have a negative influence because it can also be limiting. That having been said, learning and accepting your limitations can help you to understand your powers better.

The hour of Jupiter

Jupiter's hour is governed by the power of expansion, be it physical or spiritual, or concerning education or travel.

This an excellent hour for casting spells to do with holidays or careers or those concerned with gaining spiritual insight and wisdom.

The hour of Mars

Mars was the Roman god of war and this planet's influence is therefore somewhat fiery and masculine, also being concerned with sexuality and drive.

This would be a good hour to cast spells linked with work or competition because the fiery nature of this planet will provide the energy that you need. On the downside, Mars' influence can bring about conflict, so, before casting such spells, be certain of what it is that you want and how it will affect others.

THE PHASES OF THE MOON

The moon's magnetic force influences the tides of the world's oceans, and because 80 per cent of our bodies consists of water, it is also thought to affect our internal balance (which may also explain how the planets can affect us physically).

Our closest neighbor in space, the moon has been worshipped by many cults and religions throughout history. The Native Americans, for instance, who often call it "Grandmother Moon," venerate it as a source of ancient wisdom and feminine intuition. Some cultures used the moon to mark one's age, so that someone who was 43 years old would be said to have lived for 559 moons (there are 13 new moons during a year).

In the Wiccan faith, the moon is linked with the year's four lunar festivals (see pages 76 to 80) and is regarded as the physical manifestation of the goddess Diana, the Roman goddess of the moon. While the sun symbolizes the masculine force that is strong and seen, the moon, on the other hand, being merely a reflection of the sun, signifies the feminine, unseen world of emotions and feelings. Its three visible phases represent the three phases of womanhood: the new moon symbolizes the virgin (or the girl); the full moon, the maiden (or the mother); and the old, or waning, moon, the crone (or the old woman). The dark moon represents death and rebirth.

TOP The tides and weather of the seasons are all controlled by the moon as it orbits our planet.

ABOVE The power of the moon also effects the balance of fluid within us which in turn effects our emotional balance.

LEFT The ever-changing cycles of the moon can have a dramatic affect on our every day lives.

RIGHT The 28-day cycle of the moon is akin to the female menstrual cycle and its three phases are also linked to the three ages of womanhood, the virgin, the maiden, and the crone.

There are many traditions connected with the new moon. In some parts of Britain, for instance, people turn small change over in their pockets when they see a new moon to ensure that their money will grow during the next month. Some people consider it bad luck to glimpse the new moon though a window, because doing so will distort its power, while many people make a wish when they see it. The period of a new moon is an excellent time to cast spells concerned with new projects or ventures.

The full moon is considered a good time to perform almost any type of magic, but especially magic concerned with love. Many Wiccan and Druidic ceremonies were performed on the night of the full moon because this is when the moon is at its most powerful (presumably it also enabled them to see what they were doing!) Because the moon represents instincts and the unseen, and these influences are at their strongest when the moon is full, I personally find this phase of the moon a powerful time to do card-readings.

BELOW The old moon is a good time to put behind you any feelings of pain or sadness, as the moon dies so will your negativity.

Because it represents the end of the lunar cycle, the phase of the waning moon is a good time to rid oneself of any unwanted feelings or memories. If you have had a run of bad luck, or are suffering emotional hurt in the wake of a bad relationship, this is the best time for cleansing and banishing any negative forces from your life.

The phase of the dark moon is not considered a good time for magic because it denotes a time to rest and prepare for what is to come. It is, however, helpful for reflection, for learning from the past, and for considering future plans, so if you are thinking about casting a spell, this would be the best time to ponder your intent.

TOP Many traditions are linked to the moon, in some parts of Britain money is turned over in the pocket when the new moon is first seen, in hope that this money will grow with the moon.

ABOVE The moon also teaches us hope of rebirth, the moon grows smaller marking the time of old age and finally disappears only to return as a new cycle begins.

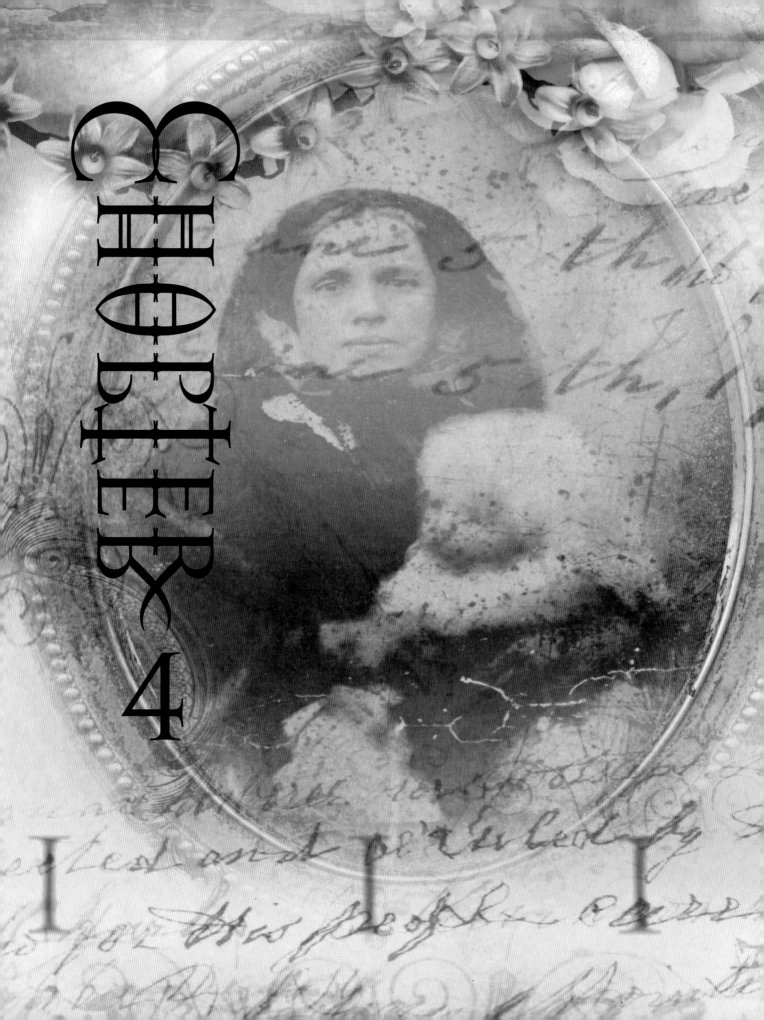

CHAPTER 4

WICCA AND THE HOME

After our early ancestors had finally stopped their nomadic wanderings and had settled down to build communities, the concept of the home began to take shape within human culture. No longer just places in which to shelter from the wind, rain, or harsh snows of winter, dwellings became almost womb-like spaces, offering safety from the perils of the outside world, not just the physical dangers of the real world, but also the unseen dangers of the spirit world. Paintings found in the earliest human cave dwellings are thought to represent the first evidence of the use of magic with which to protect a home and its inhabitants.

Household traditions

In many cultures, the building of a new home was steeped in magical ceremony and tradition. Offerings of fruit and sacrifices of fresh meat would be made to the God and Goddess to ensure that the home would be blessed. Fresh eggs later replaced animal sacrifices and were either built into the walls or broken over the foundations as a form of blessing. In some parts of Britain, horses' heads were buried under the floor to protect against the "Night Mare", the mythical horse that carried evil dreams from the spirit world to haunt the sleep of humans. Iron was also used as a form of protection against evil, and broken iron tools and weapons have been found inside the walls of old houses across Europe.

ABOVE *Bits of iron or broken iron tools were often placed in the foundations of houses to protect the occupants from evil.*

Another practice was the carving of protective symbols into doorjambs to ward off evil. Although these symbols would have included the pentagram, due to the Christian-led persecution of witches, they would have been accompanied by other symbols (possibly runic) to disguise their true magical purpose. These witches' posts were used to protect not only the home, but livestock installed in outbuildings, too. (I have seen evidence of this on the farm that I grew up on, as well as on old gateposts—the protective symbols in such cases acting as a form of boundary protection for the entire farm.)

For as long as it has existed, Wiccan magic has been used to protect the home. The traditional village witch would cleanse a house of evil spirits using spells or charms, at the same time probably sharing with the woman of the house a few ideas on good house-keeping and basic hygiene which, when combined with

her medical knowledge, would help to reduce the incidence of disease and keep mortality rates low within her community.

The use of magic to cleanse and protect the home is therefore as old as human civilization and continues to be practiced throughout the world today, with ministers of most modern faiths still occasionally being called upon to perform blessings and exorcisms in the homes of members of their congregations.

The erection of ornamental roof finials, which was common in Britain until World War II, is a faint echo of the Anglo-Saxon tradition of placing antlers on the peaks of houses to appease the Horned God; many can still be seen today. The Eastern principles of Vastu and, perhaps more notably, Feng Shui, have become more widespread in the West in recent years, too. Although these tend to focus more on balancing and harmonizing the energies that flow around us, they are thought by many to greatly improve the quality of the home and of domestic life. This chapter explains how you can use magic to do the same.

ABOVE Cleansing ceremonies can help reduce the effects of any negative energy that might be lurking within your home.

BELOW The use of roof finials on houses and gargoyles on churches both stem from ancient forms of protection—these can still be seen in many parts of Britain and Europe.

BELOW Magic has been used for centuries to protect the home, the Chinese principles of Feng Shui have become extremely popular in recent years.

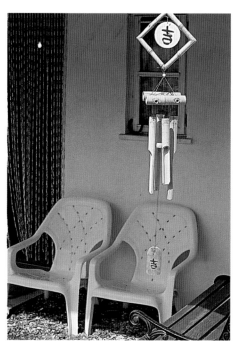

ABOVE Magic shouldn't just be used to protect your home but to help balance energies within it.

Iron: the metal of the gods

Because some cultures believed that the bones of the gods were made of iron, iron has long been considered the most magical of all metals. The Nordic war and defender god Tyr was always depicted carrying an iron sword, as were Ares and Mars, respectively the Greek and Roman gods of war. These magical weapons symbolized the gods' strength and endurance, and carrying a piece of iron was thought to bestow these qualities on a person. In China, iron was regarded as the most effective weapon against dragons, and pieces of iron were thrown into pools where dragons were believed to live, to scare them into flying away.

The original source of this metal was the iron that was found in meteorites that had fallen to Earth, the weapons and tools that were made from these meteorites being found to be far superior to their bronze counterparts. (It seemed that iron was truly a gift from the gods, and this explains the origins of numerous legends telling of magical swords and weapons forged from fallen stars.) Having no protection against this superior metal, the Neolithic peoples of the Bronze Age were driven off to the more inhospitable areas of the planet, where they eventually died out, subsequently, according to legend, evolving into fairies, elves, goblins, and a whole host of other little monsters. This is why iron has long been used as a form of magical protection against evil, and in parts of Europe an iron spike would be hammered into the ground in front of a house to guard against the forces of darkness.

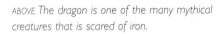

ABOVE The dragon is one of the many mythical creatures that is scared of iron.

BELOW The first iron to be discovered by man fell to earth in the form of meteorites—iron really was a gift from the heavens.

The craftsmen who were able to forge this metal were thought to be powerful magicians who, in Graeco-Roman belief, received their skills from Hephaestus (Vulcan), the son of Zeus (Jupiter) and Hera (Juno) and the god of fire and metalworking who protected those who shared his craft. Hephaestus took his mother's side when she argued with his father, causing the enraged Zeus to cast him out of the heavens. Hephaestus fell for nine days and, although saved from death by the people of Lemnos, broke his leg and limped thereafter.

In British mythology, Hephaestus was equated with Weyland (or Wayland, called Voland in Norse mythology), the god of smiths and smith to the gods (according to some early Arthurian legends, Weyland was the smith who forged Excalibur). Weyland also walked with a limp, as a result of an injury inflicted by King Nihud. A number of ancient British sites were believed to have been the location of Weyland's forge, most notably Wayland's Smithy in Wiltshire, it being said that any horses left there overnight would be shod by morning.

Blacksmiths who limped (and many were injured through working with hot and heavy metals) were said to bear the mark of Weyland, while the forge was considered a place of magic, where the four elements of air, fire, water, and earth united to create iron from rocks. The village forge was, until relatively recently, so highly valued that it was sometimes hidden outside the village in case of attack, giving rise to many legends telling of dwarves who mined and forged iron in their high mountain smithies.

In times past, marriage ceremonies were often carried out over the blacksmith's anvil (as they still are at Gretna Green, in the Scottish borders, where many young lovers once eloped in order to get married), while the making of the sign of the cross at the end of the ceremony to seal the union of the happy couple, although now a Christian symbol, is ultimately derived from the making of the sign of the hammer, the symbol of Thor (the Nordic god of thunder, who was also linked with blacksmiths).

ABOVE The blacksmith's forge was considered a magical place where the elements of earth, air, fire, and water all came together to turn rocks into weapons and tools.

CLEANING AND CLEANSING

Cleaning and cleansing rituals should be carried out when you first move into a new house or aparment, but if you have lived at your present address for some time and don't intend to move, you can still use magic to cleanse your home of any spirits and negative energies.

MAGICAL TIPS FOR MOVING HOME

If you are about to move house or apartment, you may be interested in a number of traditions that are said to ensure that you will enjoy prosperity and happiness in your new home.

Before you move in, first clean your new home from top to bottom and then scatter some dirt from your old home in each of the four corners of your new place. This should make your new home as happy as your last (which is fine if you were happy in your old home, but I wouldn't recommend doing this if you weren't). Another option is to use some dirt from your family home (as long as you got on with your family when you were living there), while an alternative is to collect some dirt from somewhere where you enjoy being alone, such as a quiet corner of a forest or park, and to scatter that.

Another tradition is to move a heavy item of furniture, such as a chair, bookcase, or table, into your new home before anything else. This is said to anchor you firmly in place, ensuring that you will be staying in your new home for a long time.

Choose whichever piece of furniture represents what you most want from your new home: a chair for relaxation, for example, a bookcase for study, a desk for work or a bed for … (well, I'm sure you get the point!)

Note that moving house on a Saturday is thought to be unlucky and means that you won't be living at your new address for very long. This is because Saturday, being traditionally the last day of the week, should be a day for endings, not beginnings.

Negativity in the home can manifest itself in many ways, causing a range of physical and psychological problems, such as headaches, depression, insomnia or nightmares, for instance. More mundane manifestations include a light fitting that keeps blowing bulbs or a doorway on which you always seem to stub your toe.

ABOVE *Cleansing of negative energy can help increase happiness and contentment within the home.*

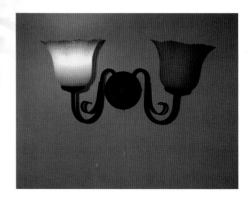

ABOVE *The effects of negativity may be almost unnoticeable, but if you look around your home you may start to see it, e.g. light bulbs that seem to keep blowing out!*

In more extreme cases, this negative energy can lead to haunting-type symptoms, in which case you may need to solicit the help of a trained minister (of whatever faith you feel comfortable with) to cleanse your home. Every home has some negative energy lurking in it somewhere, but in most instances the effects are thankfully quite subtle, and often almost unnoticeable.

RIGHT Keeping your home free of clutter not only improves the look of the place but also encourages the flow of energy and prevents it from building up and causing problems.

LEFTNegative energy can collect in doorways, causing you to trip or stub your toes.

Just as many people think of their cars as having a personality, so your home has a personality, one that is made up of the energies and memories of the people who lived there before you. You may not have a problem with your home's personality (and, indeed, some people consider it something to be treasured and not driven away by cleansing), but if you do, cleaning and ridding it of clutter is an important first step in ridding your home of negative energy. This will, in addition, not only create a more harmonious living space, but will also help you to develop a connection with your home.

BELOW Traditionally, the first thing you should move into a new home is a heavy item of furniture. This is supposed to create a stable environment and mean you will be there a long time.

Household spirits

The presence of a spirit in the home is often thought to be an unpleasant, even dangerous, phenomenon. Although this is certainly true in some cases, many cultures considered it a positive thing, not something to be feared. Indeed, certain spirits were often encouraged to enter the home because it was believed that they would provide protection and good luck.

The banshees of Ireland and parts of Scotland were thought to be domestic spirits that watched over and protected the family with whom they lived. Although these wailing spirits were often linked with death, it was said that they would only wail as an expression of sadness at the death of a family member. Similarly, in a traditional Scottish belief, brownies, luck-bringing, fairy-type creatures, would befriend a family and move into their home, food often being left out for them after the rest of the family had gone to bed.

The ancient Romans welcomed the presence of spirits in their homes, too, notably the Lares, or Penates, who were believed to be the spirits of the family's ancestors. They were often consulted on the household's day-to-day matters and offerings of flour, dried fruit, and salt were made in their honor.

A tradition that is still practiced in some parts of Britain is the placing of a spirit house, a miniature house made of china or brass and decorated with glass or crystals, above the fireplace. This provides a spirit with a home if it wanders into the house and decides to stay, its presence then being thought to protect the home from invasion by other spirits.

ABOVE Horseshoes can still be seen nailed to front doors for good luck and protection against evil spirits. Traditionally the horseshoe was nailed with the two ends pointing upward, to prevent the luck from running out.

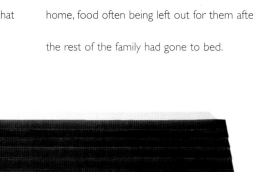

LEFT Model or china houses kept above the fireplace stems from the tradition of the spirit house.

After you have cleaned your home and have thrown out any junk that was cluttering it up, the next step is to cleanse it magically.

Although there are many ceremonies and chants that you could use, a spell that you could try in the first instance is one adapted from the ceremony detailed in Chapter 1, which you should follow (see pages 32 to 35) to the point at which you have bowed to the four points of the compass. Now pick up a white candle and again bow to the four compass points. Each time you do so, say, "Power of the [state the name of the direction] and the element of [state the name of the element of that direction], bless this candle with the power of the Goddess to cleanse my home of darkness!"

Then place the candle in front of you and light it, saying, "I light this candle as the light of the Goddess."

Relax and focus on the light of the candle. Imagine that light expanding and filling the circle around you, then hold that image and let its power grow in your mind until you feel it start to reach its peak.

Now breathe out gently over the candle, making sure that you don't blow it out, and say, "Let the light of the Goddess …"

Take another breath and say, "… shine throughout my home!"

Then, taking one last breath, say, "In the name of the Goddess, shadows begone!" As you say "shadows begone!" blow out the candle and imagine the circle of light expanding to fill your

ABOVE Candles, especially if they are scented, can help to cleanse and create the right mood within your home.

home, pushing any shadows outward as it does so.

Now finish casting the spell in the usual way.

Another way of casting this spell, and one that can work especially well if you live in a large house or are new to spell-casting, is to focus on one room only. Although there are no physical limits in magic, a room is a considerably smaller area to cleanse than a house, and you may therefore find it easier to cleanse a room at a time. Many witches perform this type of spell once a month on the full moon, when the power of the Goddess is at its strongest. You may similarly want to cast this spell every full moon if you find that it makes your home feel a better place.

BELOW Rather than trying to cleanse all your home at once, try working with one room at a time.

PROTECTION AND PROSPERITY

Once you have cleansed your home, you must try to prevent any more spirits or negative energies from entering it. There are a number of ways of warding off negativity, one of the more popular being to hang a pair of crossed brooms over the fireplace or doorway.

Another method is to fill an old leather shoe or boot with some salt, pins, and scissors and then to add such herbs as rosemary and basil or, alternatively, plants like ferns or mistletoe. Once you've filled the shoe or boot, hang it somewhere in your home, preferably out of sight (attics and basements are the best spots, or else the backs of wardrobes).

ABOVE *Pokers are yet another form of iron protection that can be used.*

SALT AND MAGIC

Salt has been vital to human survival over the millennia, being our first antiseptic and food preservative before the invention of the icebox and the canning process. Despite all of the advances in science, salt is still used for cleaning eating and cooking utensils in many parts of the world; many dentists continue to recommend gargling with salt water to improve oral hygiene; while adding salt to bath water is a well-known cure for aches and muscle tension.

The ancient Romans valued salt most highly and often paid their soldiers with it, hence the expression "worth his salt". It is said to derive its name from Salus, the Roman goddess of health (whom the ancient Greeks called Hygeia), and the spilling of salt was thought to

BELOW *Shoes placed by doors, fireplaces, and windows are thought to protect these points of entry from evil forces.*

bring bad luck, that is, unless it was thrown over the left shoulder with the right hand, and preferably into a fast-flowing river.

This Roman tradition is echoed in Leonardo da Vinci's painting of *The Last Supper*, in which Judas Iscariot has knocked over the saltcellar with his arm, thereby symbolizing bad luck and treachery.

Salt is also used by the Roman Catholic Church in the baptism of children, and, until relatively recently, was placed in coffins to ward off the powers of evil, salt being thought to represent the incorruptible and pure, such as the "salt of the earth".

You could also make a copy of the old Druidic symbol for the hearth and home (right) and hang it over the fireplace, or anywhere else, although it works best in a communal area or somewhere that represents the heart of your home.

On the witches' wheel (below right), the darkest quarter is that of west to north, which is linked with death and long, dark nights. This area of your home is the most open to negative forces and should therefore be protected. Although these forces can seep in through the brickwork, they can also enter through such openings as doors, windows and fireplaces (the latter, of course, being Father Christmas' favorite entry point).

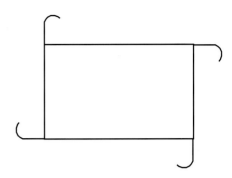

ABOVE This is an old Druidic symbol of the home and it is believed to encourage prosperity.

BELOW Salt has long been used for cleaning and cleansing, the Romans valued it so highly they often paid their soldiers with it, hence the expression "worth his salt!".

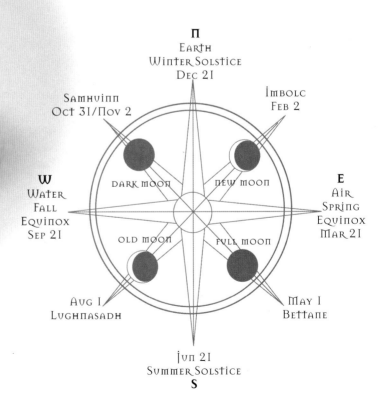

ABOVE The teachings and lesson of the witches' wheel can also be applied to the home ensuring health and happiness.

Front and back doors are the thresholds to our homes, and spirits and negative energies can pass through them just as easily as we do. To fend them off, simply sprinkle a line of salt across the doorway, preferably placing a doormat or carpet over the top. You could also position a pair of crossed pins under a doormat or carpet in front of the door. The best-known warder-off of evil is a horseshoe, but hammering three iron nails, with one pointing upward, into the front of a door will also protect against fairies and evil spirits.

Iron and mirrors can be used for banishment, too and, because spirits are believed to be frightened of their own reflections, positioning mirrors so that they face the front door or hang on either side of the hallway will scare them away.

ABOVE Placing pins or sharp iron tools under the carpet in front of doors is another use of iron as a form of protection.

ABOVE Mirrors placed by doorways are thought to frighten away evil spirits who are believed to be scared of their own reflections.

RIGHT Horseshoes are a common sight on doors throughout Britain.

Because of their obvious link with doors, keys can also be used to prevent negative forces from entering your home, as follows. Take a bunch of old keys, one for each door in your dwelling, but not ones that will open any locks or doors in your house. Starting with the back door, touch the door with every key in turn, each time saying:

"Lock out thieves in the night,

Lock out thieves in the light,

Lock out thieves out of sight."

Repeat the procedure for every door in your home, ending with the front door. Then tie the keys together with a red ribbon and hang them over the front door.

Certain vegetables and herbs can form a barrier against evil, too. A bunch of onions or garlic hung on a door is thought to protect against most forms of evil, while a bag containing a mixture of rosemary, basil and dill hung on, or near, the front door will serve as general protection.

"Lock out thieves in the night, Lock out thieves in the light, Lock out thieves out of sight."

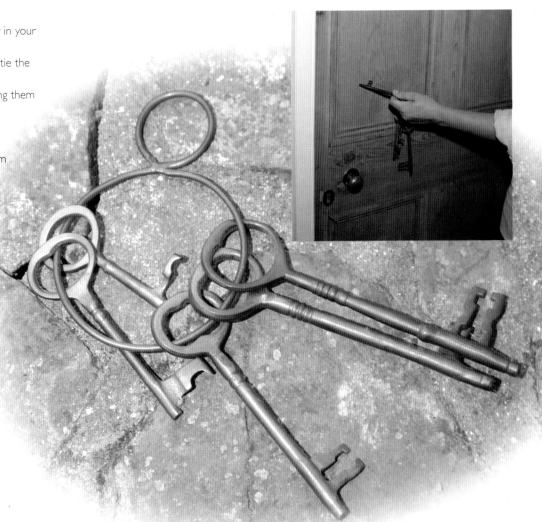

LEFT *Bags filled with herbs hung on or near doors, windows, and other openings can be an alternative to iron as a protection.*

ABOVE *Candle magic (like crystal magic) relies on color symbolism and can cleanse, protect or bless a home.*

Although many of the ways of protecting doors outlined above will protect windows equally well, a few methods work on windows only. A popular one is drawing a pentagram on the window, either in the condensation that sometimes forms on windowpanes in the mornings, or by wetting your finger with a little saltwater and drawing the sign with that. Placing certain items on a windowsill, such as bowls filled with seashells or protective crystals like amber, calcite, obsidian, jade, jasper, or serpentine, will also protect a window, as will any brass or iron ornament. Sun-catchers or stained-glass decorations hung in a window will not only decorate the window space and, in the latter case, cast a pleasing light into the room, but will help to block and break up negative energy.

You could also try some candle magic by adapting the ceremony detailed above for cleansing (see page 96). This time, use a blue candle (blue being a feminine and protective color), and when you bow to the four corners to empower it, say, "Power of the [state the name of the direction] and the element of [state the name of the element], bless this candle in the name of the Goddess to protect my home from darkness."

ABOVE *Sun-catchers are thought to encourage air spirits to bless your windows and therefore protect these areas for negative forces.*

Then place the candle in front of you and say, "I light this candle as the power of the Goddess" and imagine its light filling the circle. Let the power build in your mind until it is close to peaking, then gently breathe out over the candle, as you do so saying, "Let the power of the Goddess …"

Take a breath and then say, "… shine throughout my home!"

Then take a final breath and say, "In the name of the Goddess, protect my home!" As you say these words, blow out the candle to finish the spell.

ABOVE Seashells and crystals placed in the window can also form a protective barrier.

Another good spell that can be used to deal with a difficult visitor (or to ward off an intruder) is a diminishing-word spell that uses a variation of the old magical power word "abracadabra", "norodardogor", to decrease the person's power. To cast the spell, picture the person in your mind's eye and say,

"To shrink his [or her] lust
And wither his dust,
Call the first,
Diminish the rest,
Whisper the last!"

Then say the word "norodargogor". Now reduce it by knocking off the first two letters (to give "rodardogor") and say this. Repeat this procedure until you are left with "or", as shown below.

"NORODARDOGOR"
"RODARDOGOR"
"DAROGOR"
"ROGOR"
"OGOR"
"OR"

You could also use "rogorodoron"—a variation of "norodardogor"—to boost your own power by starting with the shortest

ABOVE Iron can again be used, but, as the window space is a visible and open area, try and use ornaments that enhance the look of the window.

version of the word and then increasing it in a similar manner. Before doing so, however, say,

> 'Lie down as dead,
>
> Then upward awaken,
>
> Raise this word
>
> Thy strength to quicken.'

Then say the word 'or', thereafter increasing it by two letters at a time, as shown below, until the last word that you say is 'rogorodoron'.

OR
ORON
DORON
RODORON
GORODORON
ROGORODORON

Although I have been familiar with the theory of this form of word magic for some time, I have only seen it used once, when an exasperated friend who was being bothered by a guy in a nightclub stood in front of him, pointing at him as she intoned the chant. The guy was so scared that he left her alone, so I guess it worked!

Once you have fully protected your home, there are certain things that you can do to increase its prosperity. For example, you could use candle magic (again follow the basic ceremony described in Chapter 1, pages 34 to 35, and also above), but this time use either a gold candle for prosperity or a green candle for love and harmony.

ABOVE Using gold-colored candles (gold being one of the colors of money!) can help increase prosperity.

You could use charms and symbols (see pages 60 to 67) to increase the prosperity of your home, too, but because magic is a personal art, rather than give you specific advice, it would be better if you found a charm or symbol that applies best to you and your circumstances. I saw many such charms being used while I was growing up in Wales, and in every case they were something personal to the householder. To give a couple of examples, a friend of mine collects model pigs and another has a little doll representing the Cartman character from the television program South Park on his mantelpiece, both of which signify abundance and plenty. Rather than pigs, you could use figures of cows or bulls (and bulls also represent strength and endurance) or even representations of dogs or cats, which, although they mainly symbolize guardianship and protection, nevertheless have a benevolent effect.

BELOW Animal charms can also help make your home happier and more productive.

Meditation and balance

Once you have cleansed and protected your home, the next step is to start balancing the elementary forces that exist within it. This can be a very effective exercise that, to coin an old phrase, can "make your house a home." All that you will need to begin with is a compass, some sheets of paper and a pen.

RIGHT You will need a reliable compass to help you identify north, south, east, and west within your home.

BELOW Applying the teachings of the witches' wheel can help make your house a home and work out the best use of rooms.

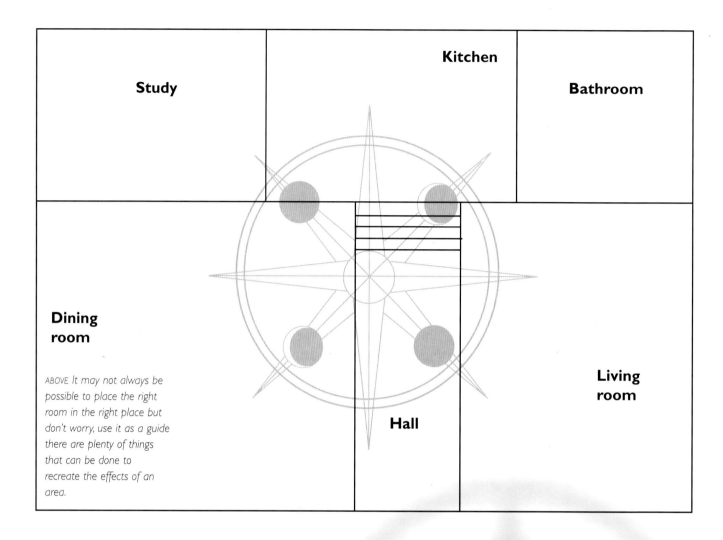

Study

Kitchen

Bathroom

Dining room

ABOVE It may not always be possible to place the right room in the right place but don't worry, use it as a guide there are plenty of things that can be done to recreate the effects of an area.

Hall

Living room

The first thing to do is to draw a plan of your house, flat or, if you share your house with others, your room. Note down what each room or area is used for, then identify north and mark the four points of the compass on your plan. As I've already explained, each point of the compass is linked with an element (see pages 46 to 48), as well as one of the eight festivals of the witches' wheel (see pages 72 to 75).

Now superimpose the witches' wheel on your plan, which should leave you with a square made up of nine sections: four representing the elements and the solar festivals, four representing the times of life and the lunar festivals, and one representing the center, or hub, of the wheel. Each of these nine sections has a unique set of influences that lend themselves to certain uses, so that, in a perfect world, you could arrange your home to enable

each room to be situated in the best place for its use. We don't live in a perfect world, however, and rearranging your home to match the witches' wheel may not be practical, yet if this is so, don't despair because there are certain alternatives open to you, as follows.

The north

Because the key words for the north are rest, wisdom and conception, this is the best area for studies and reading rooms, especially if they are used for research. Due to its links with the element of earth, the north is also a good place in which to store and display items that denote wealth and success.

The earthy nature of this area makes it ideal for kitchens, too, although you may want to add a fire element to make it a better cooking area.

BELOW Bedrooms work well in the north, especially if you enjoy a restful night's sleep, though you may want to add a water element if you like to dream.

Because the north can be a restful area, you could also site bedrooms or living rooms in it, although you may find that you need to add a water element to introduce a more relaxing and reflective atmosphere. (If you feel uncomfortable about using the north as a sleeping area, due to its association with winter and death, try not to worry, because it is not a place of endings, but beginnings.) You could also site a workroom or office here, but may be advised to add extra fire or air elements to promote creativity and combat the north's restful influence.

ABOVE The earthy nature of kitchens means that they can also be placed in the north, but you may want to try fire or air to boast creative influences.

RIGHT The north is the place of endings and beginnings, this can be linked to restful sleep but also the death and rebirth, so those of a nervous disposition may not feel comfortable with this.

The north-east

The keywords for this area are inspiration, birth and dependence, making the north-east best suited to playrooms, games rooms (which link one with one's inner child) or any room associated with young children. If you enjoy playing computer games or constructing model railways, these purposes are similarly well served by the north-eastern section.

Although this area can be used for workrooms, any inspirational benefit may be counteracted by the playful nature associated with this direction, so add some fire elements to encourage drive, and maybe an earth element to help to keep you grounded.

Bedrooms (especially children's bedrooms) can be sited in this area, but, because difficulties in falling asleep may result, make such spaces more relaxing by introducing the element of water.

BELOW Linked to childhood and new beginnings this is the best area for children's rooms or play rooms (even if the children are big boys who need a room for model railways or playing computer games).

The East

The keywords associated with the east are life, renewal and germination. This area is best used for morning or breakfast rooms, but can also be a good place for workrooms, such as kitchens and offices, although you may need to add fire and earth elements to contribute drive and grounding.

Like the north-east, because it doesn't aid sleep, this direction is rather unsuitable for bedrooms, although you could add a water element to encourage relaxation and then go one step further and introduce an earth element to prevent your mind from wandering while you are slumbering.

Depending on how relaxing you want it to be, you could site your bathroom in this area, again adding a water element to promote the ability to unwind. However, if your household is large, try not to make the bathroom too relaxing, because this could lead to family members spending too much time in the bath.

ABOVE The east can be a good area for family kitchens, the element of air will ensure lively communication, especially over breakfast!

BELOW Home offices can also work here—with new ideas coming thick and fast you may need to add an earth element to keep you grounded.

The south-east

The keywords for the south-east are strength, youth, and independence. Because the elements of air and fire combine here, this area is best used as an office or workspace. Because the combination of air and fire can create an almost explosive atmosphere, however, you may need to add an earth element to provide some grounding, while the addition of a water element could offer a restful focal point (but keep it small to ensure that it doesn't distract you from your work).

The south-east is not that good an area for a bedroom, if your primary use for it will be for sleeping (given the keywords for this area, an alternative use will, no doubt, spring to mind), and I'd advise adding an earth or water element to encourage relaxation (after all, we all need to sleep at some point).

The independent nature of the south-east makes it inadvisable to use this area as a communal space, such as a living or dining room, because tempers are likely to flare. Even if you add a mitigating water element, you may still find that territorial instincts take over within this area.

Although you could site a bathroom in the south-east, you may find yourself competing with other family members to use it, so I'd again advocate installing a water element to imbue this area with some calmness.

TOP RIGHT The combination of air and fire, causing creativity and drive, makes this a good place for offices.

RIGHT Living rooms are not well suited for this area, as it can have an independent nature about it that can lead to arguments.

The south

The keywords for the south are spirit, power, and change. Although this area is excellent for offices and workspaces, you may need to add an earth element to keep your feet planted firmly on the ground and to prevent you from getting ahead of yourself.

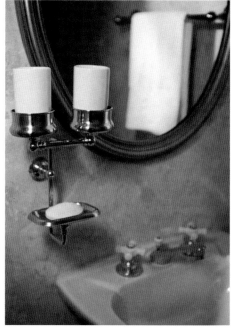

The south is not a good area for bathrooms, family rooms, or bedrooms because its fiery nature could lead to arguments and sleeplessness (but because the south is associated with the time of mating on the witches' wheel, it does depend on your bedroom's primary purpose). Although you can counteract these influences with water and earth elements to some extent, the south still remains an area that is not suited to rest and relaxation.

ABOVE If you need to make this a more relaxing area try adding an extra earth element, because the south is linked to fire; adding water just creates steam. For this reason bathrooms (like living rooms!) shouldn't really be placed here!

LEFT The fiery nature of the south makes it a bad area for rest and relaxation, so kitchens, offices, and works rooms of any kind would work better here.

The south-west

The keywords for the south-west are insight, family, and dependence. This is the best place for family rooms and communal areas because the fire element of the south is cooled by the water element of the west. Although this combination can sometimes create steam (that is, arguments), this area offers some patience and relaxation, which means that any disputes should be short-lived and relatively minor.

The south-west can be suitable for workrooms, but the influence of water's dreamy nature may cause difficulties when it comes to remaining focused on a task. Kitchens—especially if they are used as family dining areas—can be sited here, but you may need to add some earth elements.

Bathrooms generally function well when situated in the south-west, but be warned that the influence of the element of fire means that you may find yourself arguing with other household members about who uses the bathroom next!

The south-west is not a very restful space, which means that although you can site living rooms here, you may find relaxation difficult, which is why this area is not that suitable for bedrooms either. If you want to introduce some relaxing vibes, however, add some water and earth elements.

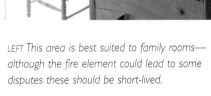

LEFT This area is best suited to family rooms—although the fire element could lead to some disputes these should be short-lived.

TOP Adding some water or earth elements could help to counteract any fiery effects of the south-west.

ABOVE Kitchens are suited to the south-west (especially if it is also used for dining!), although, if they are placed here, you might have to add some earth elements to help keep the room grounded.

The West

The keywords for the west are reflection, compassion, and emotions. Because this area has a watery nature, it is best suited to bathrooms, but living rooms (especially if you like listening to relaxing music), and bedrooms are equally well placed here because of the west's relaxing properties.

Bedrooms that are sited in the west can offer dream-filled sleep, which shouldn't usually present a problem because the dreams will be relaxing ones, but if a more restful type of sleep is required, try adding an earth element.

Communal rooms could work well in the west, but the influence of water may have a dreamy, distracting effect, which you could mitigate by introducing some fire, and maybe earth, elements.

Workrooms are unsuited to a western situation, but if this is unavoidable, including plenty of fire elements should counteract any undesirable influences. Because water and fire create steam, however, provide some stability by adding an earth element.

ABOVE The watery nature of the west makes it a perfect area for bathrooms!

BELOW Bedrooms can work well here, but it can have a reflective effect that could cause your mind to dream and this might not suit everyone, if so try an earth element to help you stay grounded.

ABOVE Living rooms also work here if you want them to be relaxing, if not, a fire or air element could help liven them up a little.

THE NORTH-WEST

The keywords for the north-west are cleansing, existence and independence. On the witches' wheel, this is the area of Samhuinn, the witches' new year, as well as the time of death, when the gateways to the spirit world are opened. If you accept that death is a part of life, you should have no problems with this area, but if the north-west's links with death and the spirit world trouble you, protect any north-western rooms, especially the walls (see pages 100 to 106 for details on how to do this). Having protected it, you can then use this area for living rooms because the combination of water and earth makes the north-west a place of relaxation and rest.

ABOVE The mix of water and earth make this area good for relaxation so living rooms are well placed here, but you may want to try fire or air to liven it up slightly.

BELOW Any room could work here just as long as you use protections and add the right combinations of elements.

Bathrooms also function well in the north-west, as do bedrooms (although not for children because they may fall prey to nightmares, see page 96), but, if the thought of sleeping in an area associated with death makes you feel uncomfortable, remember that negative forces are usually powerless if you have no fear of them, and that you will, in any case, be safe if you have protected the area. If using this area as a bedroom results in the experiencing of dream-filled nights, try placing a symbol of a horse in the room. The horse, which is traditionally linked with the goddesses Rhiannon and Epona and is thought to be the animal that opens and closes the gates of the other world, has been used to encourage good sleeping patterns for centuries, but because it also

represents the cycle of life and death, it can act as a protective form of appeasement.

You can safely site any other types of room, including offices and kitchens, in the north-west, as long as you use the correct balance of elements to counteract any of this area's unwanted effects.

ABOVE Bedrooms work well here, but as this area is linked with death, you may not feel comfortable sleeping here—if you use protections you shouldn't have any problems.

The center

As the hub of the witches' wheel, the center is the area where all of the lessons and influences of the directions combine. As the center of your home, it is unlikely that this area would be practical for use as a room and, in any case, is probably a hallway or stairwell.

The center is nevertheless very important because the life energy of the witches' wheel doesn't simply flow clockwise around the rim, but also across the hub, linking opposing points on the wheel. The central area should therefore be kept tidy and free of clutter in order to encourage the flow of energy. You may, however, want to place items (perhaps photographs of friends or family members or ornaments that remind you of happy times) representing the happiness and prosperity that you would like to exist within your home at its center. If so, remember not to overdo it in case you restrict the flow of energy with clutter.

ABOVE This area of the home is often taken up by hallways and stairs and is normally overlooked, yet the correct balancing of this area will affect every area of your home.

ABOVE The center is where all energies and lessons combine and flow, so it is important to keep this area uncluttered. The addition of a mirror helps redirect energy.

ABOVE As the center, you might want to fill this area with photos or mementoes of your family.

Making elemental adjustments

If you find that the rooms of your home are sited in the wrong areas, but moving them isn't an option, don't worry too much because there are certain things that you can do to help to remedy this problem, namely using elemental or visual items to recreate the influences of a room's correct area.

As a general rule of thumb, look at a room's ideal area on the witches' wheel, think about the time of year with which it is linked, and then use anything that you associate with that time of year to recreate the effects of the area. Further guidance is given.

BELOW If you want to create the effects of the north try using large items of heavy wooden furniture.

Recreating the effects of the north

To recreate the effects of the north, you could use the element of earth, which is symbolized by heavy, solid items of furniture, especially bookcases, for example, or items of wealth. You could also use such plant symbols as mistletoe or pine cones, both of which are associated with winter and therefore with the north. Certain creatures can be linked with the north, too. The bear, for instance, is a creature that returns to its cave, the symbolic womb of Mother Nature, to hibernate during the long winter months, while, although birds normally represent air, the robin—still a popular subject for Christmas cards—has long been associated with the winter solstice.

Recreating the effects of the north-east

To recreate the effects of the north-east, you could try combining the elements of earth and air, both of which are represented by the robin. You could also use an object that symbolizes the festival of Imbolc, such as an image of the goddess Bridget, the goddess of motherhood. Flowers, like daffodils and snowdrops, can help to replicate the influence of the north-east, too.

Recreating the effects of the east

To recreate the effects of the east, you could focus on the element of air, which is symbolized by birds, feathers, or photographs of skyscapes, especially if they show the early morning dawn. Because smell is airborne, you could also use air-fresheners, oil-burners or incense sticks, while further alternatives include wind chimes or sun-catchers. An animal that is linked with the spring, the east's time of year, is the hare, but a rabbit would also be suitable, because it has come to share its long-eared cousin's symbolic significance.

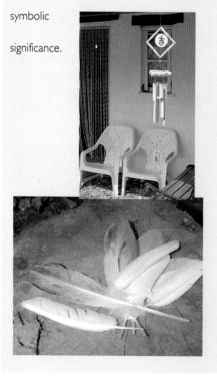

Recreating the effects of the south-east

To recreate the effects of the south-east, you could combine the elements of air and fire, which are symbolized, for example, by gold-colored mirrors or sun-catchers. Because the gateway to the spirit world opens at Beltane, the south-east's time of year, you could also use images of such creatures as horses or swans (the latter represented the soul in the belief of Celtic Europe) as symbolic tools.

Recreating the effects of the south

To recreate the effects of the south, you could use the element of fire, which is symbolized, for instance, by bright colors, electrical items, images of the sun and yellow or gold-colored candles or crystals. You could alternatively use anything linked with summer, such as photographs of summer holidays or landscapes.

RECREATING THE EFFECTS OF THE SOUTH-WEST

To recreate the effects of the south-west, try combining the elements of fire and water, which can be symbolically represented by water-filled bowls topped with floating candles or photographs of the sun setting over the ocean. You could also use symbolic objects that represent this time of year: bowls of fruit or dried flowers, for instance, for in many parts of the world this is the time of the first harvest, when nature's bounty is plentiful.

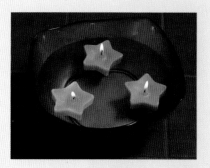

RECREATING THE EFFECTS OF THE WEST

One idea for recreating the effects of the west is to use the element of water, which is symbolized, for instance, by water features and seashells, images of fishes or photographs of rivers, seas, and boats. Because the west is linked with the Goddess, you could, alternatively, use images of the moon, silver ornaments or mirrors. This is also the time of fall and the end of harvest, which can be symbolically represented by bowls filled with nuts.

RECREATING THE EFFECTS OF THE NORTH-WEST

To replicate the effects of the north-west, combine the elements of water and earth, but be mindful of its links with death and the spirit world, and take care when recreating this area. You could alternatively use images of horses or swans (see page 121) or such creatures as cranes (which, in the belief of Celtic Europe, were thought to carry the soul to the spirit world, as well as to wait on and guard the souls of the living) or squirrels, which represent the bridge between this world and the other world.

ROOMS AND THE ELEMENTS

Some elements work best in certain rooms, so that no matter where a room is sited, the correct use of these elements can help it to function better.

Although representatives of each of the four elements (all positioned so that they face the correct direction) should be present in a room, some of them should dominate the room in accordance with its primary use, as outlined below.

Kitchens

The kitchen combines work with creativity and the stability of the family or home. The elements that should be present in a kitchen are fire, air, or earth, their dominance depending on the primary role that the kitchen plays within your home.

Dining rooms

Dining rooms are generally communal areas, and air is therefore the best dominant element because it promotes lively communication. Depending on the nature of your home life, however, you may want to add an earth element for extra stability or a water element for a more relaxing area in which to eat.

Living rooms

We tend to relax and unwind in living rooms, making water the best dominant element, but if your living room is a communal area, you may want to incorporate an extra earth element to encourage family stability or an air element to boost communication. Take care when adding such elements, however, because they may disrupt your ability to relax.

Offices and studies

Offices are areas of work and creativity, so try using the element of fire for work and drive, combined with a representative of the element of air for creation and inspiration. If your work involves studying or research, you could add an earth element, but don't let it dominate the room, because its influence may be so restful that it distracts you from your work.

Earth elements are good to include in studies because they represent knowledge. If you use your study for work-related research or creativity, you may want to add an air or fire element, but make sure that it does not dominate the room because it could again distract you.

Bedrooms

Bedrooms are where we relax and sleep, but while the element of water encourages relaxation, it can also trigger dreams, which you may find a problem. If you do, try adding an earth element, but make sure that it is a small one because earth and water are the elements that are linked with Samhuinn, which is in turn associated with death, a connection that may make you feel uncomfortable if you have a nervous disposition. If the bedroom is a child's room, air elements will work well because they help to boost the creative thought processes that all children need for healthy development, but take care not to overdo their inclusion because they could cause your child to have sleepless nights.

Bathrooms

Water is the best element to use in a bathroom because it will reinforce the room's relaxing nature, as will the addition of an earth element, especially if you enjoy reading in the bath.

BEING IN YOUR ELEMENT

Whatever the room, or its position in your home, try to strike the correct balance of elements within it. To reiterate, every room should contain representatives of each of the four elements positioned at the right points in the room (that is, earth in the north, air in the east, fire in the south and water in the west). The room's function will dictate the element, or elements, that should dominate the room

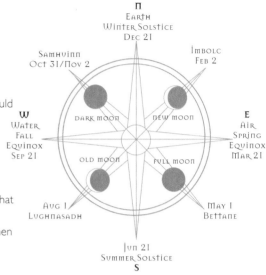

Although the examples and solutions given above can help you to balance your home, in order to ascertain what works best for you, you may need to meditate and spend some time getting to know your home. Some of us are more comfortable with certain elements, and you may need to experiment a little to find the ones that work best with you. Don't forget that your star sign is linked with an element and that you may therefore feel most comfortable when this element is dominant.

Remember that your home is your personal space. If something makes you feel safe, then use it! If something makes you feel happy, use it! If, on the other hand, something makes you feel upset or causes you distress, get rid of it!

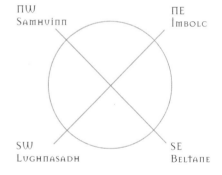

Happy Spell-Casting!

Magic is a personal art, and although the subjects discussed in this book can help to open your eyes to a much wider, more magical, world, this is only the tip of the iceberg.

My final words are those of the most important Wiccan commandment:

"Do unto others as you would have done unto you!"

Remember to use whatever you learn to help, not hinder, others. Take care and happy spell-casting!

Acknowledgments

My sincere gratitude to Jon Dee for explaining the finer points of the "bottom on the seat" method of writing, and for his help and friendship.

My thanks go to Damian, Baily, and Claire, three witches with attitude who help me understand myself. Also thanks to Joasia, Lillian, Jackie, Louie, Paula, and Julia for their love and support through difficult times.

Last, but by no means least, I would like to thank my housemates Owen, Rob, Howard, Dicky, Dave, and everyone at number 61.

Picture Credits

Star sign, sun, moon, and element illustrations by David Ashby

Photographs p 9 & 25 by Colin Bowling

Pictures pp 10, 21t, 22br, 25t, 30bl, 31, 32br, 33, 36, 37t, 39bl, 45b, 46, 47t, 49, 51b, 53, 56t, 56c(2) 67b, 73br, 68br, 74br, 75, 76t, 79br, 80tr,

82tr, 83br, 94br, 102tr, 103br, 116lc, 116br, 118, 119t, 121b, © Getty Images

Pictures pp 7, 13, 14, 15, 16, 17, 18, 19, 20, 21b, 22tr, 24, 34, 35, 37c, 37b, 38, 39tr, 40, 41, 42, 43, 44, 45t, 47b, 48, 50, 51t, 52, 55, 56c(1), 56b, 58, 63, 64, 65, 66, 67t, 68tr, 73bl, 73bc, 74tr, 74bl,

76b, 77, 78, 79tl, 80bl, 81, 82bl, 83tl, 90, 91, 92, 93, 94tl, 99, 100, 101, 102bl, 103tl, 104, 105, 108, 109, 110, 111, 112, 116tl, 117, 119b, 120, 121t, 122, © Stockbyte

(where b = bottom, t = top, l = left, c = center, r = right)